simply
pottery

DATE DUE

simply
pottery

A PRACTICAL COURSE IN
BASIC POTTERY TECHNIQUES

SARA PEARCH

with text by Geraldine Christy

Watson-Guptill Publications

New York

For Steven, Thomas, and Alexandra
with all my love

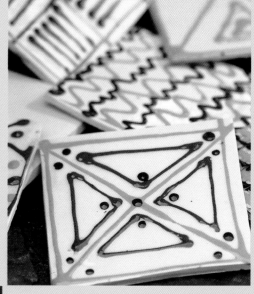

A QUINTET BOOK

First published in the United States in 1998 by
Watson-Guptill Publications
1515 Broadway
New York, NY 10036

ISBN 0-8230-4837-3

Library of Congress Catalog Card Number 98-60565

This book was designed and produced by
Quintet Publishing Limited
6 Blundell Street
London N7 9BH

Creative Director: Richard Dewing
Art Director: Silke Braun
Designer: Isobel Gillam
Project Editor: Toria Leitch
Editor: Rosie Hankin
Photographer: John Melville

Typeset in Great Britain by
Central Southern Typesetters, Eastbourne
Manufactured in Singapore by
Pica Colour Separation Overseas (Pte) Ltd
Printed in China by Leefung-Asco Printers Trading Limited

PUBLISHERS NOTE

Always follow the instructions and safety procedures
outlined in the text. As far as the techniques and
methods mentioned in this book are concerned, all
statements, information, and advice given here are
believed to be accurate. However, neither the author,
copyright holder, nor the publisher can accept any legal
liability.

contents

introduction

Clay is a marvelous material to work with and pottery is a craft that involves a total hands-on experience. Pottery has something enjoyable to offer everyone whatever their age and level of expertise, from child to adult, from beginner to fine artist-craftsperson. It involves a complete creative process as you select and prepare your material, mold and guide it into shape, apply pattern and perhaps color, then finally add a protective surface to produce a beautiful and functional item.

This book introduces you to the basic techniques of building pots with clay, shows you many different decorative effects, and explains about firing and glazing. It offers a wide range of pottery projects that are fun to make and presents ideas that you can adapt to suit your own designs as you progress.

The projects are also planned to emphasize all the five senses, but especially touch – it is through your hands that you can feel the clay respond as you work it into the sort of shape you wish to form.

Pottery also involves developing your visual awareness – closely observing the shape as the pot grows, checking that designs are symmetrical, and planning decoration and color that will enhance the pot. There are projects here that lead directly to interesting sounds, such as the rainbow chimes, or to the delicate perfume of potpourri in a pomander, and, of course, to the taste of delicious foods and drink served on platters or in bowls and mugs that you have made yourself.

Children will enjoy making the smaller pieces such as the mobile, tree decorations, and ocarina hand flute, while there is something for adults of all abilities from pottery gift boxes, buttons, and beads, through getting to grips with turning plates and jugs on the wheel.

Before you start, however, make sure that you take in all the advice on safety. Do not be frightened by it – it is there to help you enjoy potting fully. Your pottery supply store can also prove to be a good source of help and advice on all aspects of making ceramics.

Important safety advice

Producing pottery involves being constantly aware that you are dealing with dangerous substances. You must take proper precautions at all times.

Clay dust can be harmful if breathed in. Even when you are cleaning out your studio or workspace, always remember to damp down the surface first to avoid inhaling dust.

If in doubt, wear a mask.

Always wear a mask when dealing with glazes and dry compounds. This applies both when you are mixing glazes and slips and when you are dealing with glaze materials. You should also wear gloves if necessary. Chemicals may contain poisonous substances that can enter the body through the skin as well as being inhaled as particles and fumes. Always read the advice on the container or package.

Do not allow any food or drink to be consumed in the working area.

Keep all harmful materials and tools in a safe place, in tightly closed containers where appropriate, out of the reach of children and animals. Do not leave children unsupervised near any pottery materials or equipment.

When you are firing pottery, make sure that you have proper air vents to take away fumes during both biscuit and glaze firing. And remember that kilns are extremely hot ovens!

equipment and materials

It is easy to get started in pottery. All you really need is a quantity of clay and the most basic of tools. This chapter outlines the essential equipment you will require and suggests suitable potter's tools, but in many cases you can substitute simple household items that involve no extra expense.

Choose a clay that is suitable for the type of work you want to produce (your pottery supply store will help you if you are not sure) then make sure that the clay is well prepared before you start. For safety's sake as much as anything, try and sort out a space to work in that can remain relatively undisturbed. This will also allow you to leave your pots when they are "resting" between stages.

hand **tools**

A glance through any pottery supply store will reveal a vast range of tools and equipment for the would-be potter. There are special tools available for every stage of a pot's progress, but you will find that you can improvise for many of them.

As you work through the projects in the book you will see that most of them need only a few basic tools. So before rushing out to buy a particular tool have a look in your kitchen, shed, or toolbox and see if you have something that would work. Browse through the catalogs at your leisure when you have a clearer idea of what you would like to make in the future after this introduction to pottery.

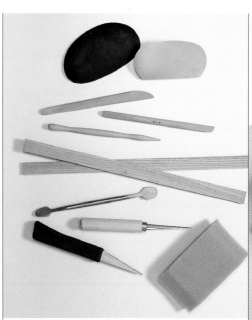

For hand building you will need a sharp knife for cutting coils or slabs of clay, rubber and metal kidneys for smoothing (or old credit cards), a variety of wooden and steel modeling tools (bits of wood and kitchen utensils will do), battens and formers, and a hole cutter. A synthetic sponge is useful for keeping surfaces clean.

For rolling out slabs of clay you will need a piece of linen or cotton cloth (sheeting), battens and formers, and a rolling pin. Cut circular slabs on a banding wheel (a rotating stand to raise your work) for accuracy.

Decorating tools can include pastry cutters, a slip bottle for trailing liquid clay, sponges for stamping, an old credit card for incising patterns, and a variety of printing sticks and clay sprigging tools (called sprigs).

When mixing glazes you need to take extra safety precautions. Wear a mask to avoid inhaling harmful fumes and overalls or an apron that can be washed easily.

Use a plastic spray bottle for spraying water onto the clay if it is drying out too much as you work.

A range of metal strip tools, turning tools, and coilers will help you turn, trim, and flute pots on the wheel. Experience will help you choose these, but you can start off with just one or two.

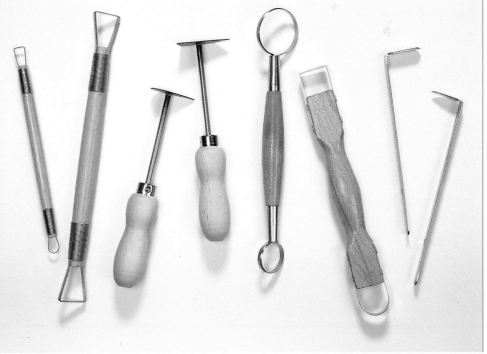

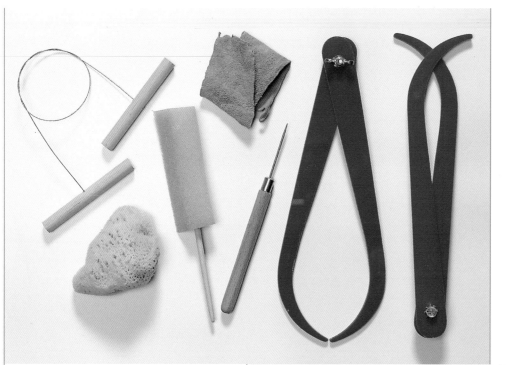

(below) Guide the shape of your pot with throwing ribs. A variety of ribs is available for different required shapes, including hooks for bellying out. You will find specific uses for bamboo or wooden turning tools and textured wood.

(above) When throwing you will need a small natural sponge to clean the wheel and tools (and for wiping off glazes and colors in unwanted areas) and a chamois for smoothing the edges of pots. A sponge on a stick is useful for soaking up excess water from a deep pot or for dabbing on slip. Use a needle gauge to trim the rim of a pot. Use a cheesewire for cutting clay and loosening the base of a pot before sliding it carefully off the wheel. Calipers will enable you to take accurate internal and external measurements.

(right) A selection of paintbrushes and glaze mops is essential for decorating and applying glaze.

equipment **and space**

Pottery is a craft that needs a fair amount of space, so if you can devote a permanent place to it, perhaps even a spare room or small studio, you will find it much easier to organize your work. Pots are often left to dry between stages and adequate shelving is essential so that they can be placed somewhere safe.

Further Equipment

There are many larger items of equipment that you will also need if you are going to take up pottery in earnest. For instance, if you are going to mix your own glazes you will need several buckets for transferring the mixtures as you strain them to the correct consistency. You will need strainers with meshes ranging from wide to fine (say, 60, 80, 100, and 120 meshes).

A reliable set of scales is also essential for weighing out clay and accurate proportions for glaze recipes. Use scoops for measuring out dry ingredients. Keep all your mixtures of glazes and slips in labeled containers.

For cutting out shapes make templates out of cardboard and cut around them with a sharp knife.

If you want to throw pots, you will probably want to buy your own wheel. Kick wheels are driven as they sound – sheer man or woman power – but it is also possible to buy motorized wheels that are not too expensive. Professional studio potters nearly always prefer an electric wheel. If you are intending to throw large items such as plates you may need batts; these are large wooden discs that you fit onto the wheel, enabling you to move any cumbersome pot off the wheel with ease.

You will need airtight storage bins where you can keep clay in damp conditions. If you want to leave pots in a damp state for further work later, a damp box or cupboard is useful. You can arrange this yourself by spraying water inside an appropriate box or cabinet.

Working Space

Flat wooden surfaces are ideal for rolling out slabs, and marble even better for kneading and wedging clay. Make sure that the surface you are using is large enough, and wipe it clean whenever necessary – dried-up bits of old clay have a habit of sticking to new pots and spoiling them.

Try to keep your work area neat, with tools kept in the same place so that you know where to find them when needed.

Make sure that you have a good source of light to work by. Natural light is obviously best, but if you are potting by electric light make sure that it is adequate.

choosing **clay**

As a natural product of the earth – indeed, it is earth – clay is a resource that is familiar to us all and draws a creative response from most people who handle it.

Clay is one of the oldest materials of use to man and consists of decomposed rock. Geologists classify clay into two groups. The first, residual or primary clays, are from rocks that have not moved from their place of origin. The second, sedimentary or secondary clays, consist of materials that have shifted or been transported by the elements away from their origins and have settled elsewhere as sediment in layers.

Sedimentary clays are used in pottery because they have acquired a looser and finer composition that makes them more malleable. Through their natural transportation these clays have picked up various minerals that further change their color and characteristics. Primary clays can occasionally be added to them if a particular property is required in pottery.

A wide range of pottery clays is available commercially. What you choose depends to some extent on what you wish to make and the sort of kiln you will be using, since each type of clay fires to a different required temperature. Your potter's suppliers will give you advice if you are uncertain.

The four main types of clay used by the novice potter are earthenware, stoneware, porcelain, and raku. All of these are available in a variety of colors, the most common being red, white, buff, and gray. The projects in this book have been made from a white earthenware clay.

Earthenware is a general-purpose clay and perhaps the most common clay used by civilizations throughout the world's history. It is suitable for throwing and for making hand-built pots. Biscuit fire at 1832°F (1000°C), glaze fire at 1904–2120°F (1040–1160°C).

Stoneware is a heavier clay with a slightly rougher texture. Also used for domestic pots, it is complemented by the application of colorful glazes. Biscuit fire at 1832°F (1000°C), glaze fire at 2192–2372°F (1200–1300°C).

Porcelain produces a finer-bodied pot. It tends to be a loose, moving clay that takes some practice in controlling, and beginners may find it a little difficult to work and throw at first. Biscuit fire at 1832°F (1000°C), glaze fire at 2264–2372°F (1240–1300°C).

Raku is a coarse clay that has a lot of grit particles or "grog" in it. It is fired at a lower temperature than other clays and can be refired to produce unusual metallic and luster effects when oxide glazes are used. Biscuit fire at 1652°F (900°C), glaze fire at 1472–1832°F (800–1000°C).

A selection of clays suitable for the novice potter (clockwise from top): Raku, Red earthenware, White earthenware, Buff stoneware, White stoneware, Porcelain.

preparing **the clay**

Before you can use a piece of clay it must be prepared properly. You must make sure that it is smooth and pliable with no lumps of grit or air pockets that might later explode in the kiln and ruin your pot. It may be necessary to soften the clay with water so that it is moist enough to use.

Clay is "kneaded" in a similar way to preparing bread dough and if you are mixing clay, perhaps combining an old leftover piece with a new larger amount, it will need to be "wedged." These processes might seem quite difficult at first as a large piece of unkneaded or unwedged clay feels heavy and awkward until it is softened, but the knack of working it is soon acquired.

When you are happy with the consistency of the clay and are sure that it contains no air bubbles, it can be stored in an airtight container where it can remain damp. If you are using the clay for throwing, roll it into balls ready for weighing before storing.

1 Work the clay on a flat surface. To soften the clay, add water and push it into the surface of the clay with your knuckles. Aim to mix a moist, pliable clay, but make sure you do not make it overwet.

2 Start working into the softened pieces of clay by punching your knuckles in, consolidating the clay into one piece.

3 Larger pieces of clay are added by wedging them. If you need to cut them from a big slab, use a cheesewire to add them slice by slice. Continue working into the clay by punching and pushing with your knuckles.

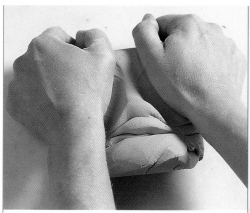

4 Start forming the clay into a roll prior to kneading it. Push the clay firmly with the palms of your hands and fold it over. Do this several times until the roll is fairly smooth and even.

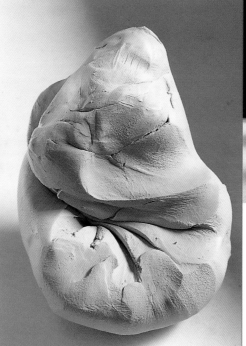

6 The kneaded clay will look something like this.

8 Cut the roll open with a cheesewire to check that all the air is out. Then cut into smaller pieces of clay that you can start rolling into balls ready for throwing. If by any chance you find a small air bubble, wedge the clay until it is even.

5 Knead the clay as you would a piece of dough. Work it with a circular movement, pushing down with one hand and pulling the clay around with the other. Continue to do this until the clay is totally malleable with an even consistency and all the air has been pushed out.

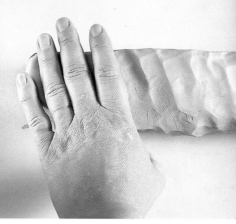

7 Finish forming the roll by slapping it with your hands to square off the edges.

9 If you wish to throw pots of a consistent size, weigh the balls of clay. They can be used immediately or stored in a damp airtight container for use later.

basic
techniques

The most important tools for making pottery are your own hands. Molding the clay into shape by pressing, supporting, and guiding it with your fingers and thumbs produces a truly unique "handmade" item. The traditional techniques of pinching and coiling clay will help you understand the plasticity of the material so that you can control it effectively to make your own designs. Learning to roll slabs evenly, to cut shapes and to join them properly will enable you to build pots of varying forms with solid bases. Mastering the skills of centering clay on the wheel and making an opening for a pot will give you the knowledge and confidence to take your pottery to the more advanced stage of throwing.

pinching

**Even the youngest of would-be potters will enjoy squeezing and pinching
a small piece of clay into a hollowed bowl shape.**

It seems to be a natural instinct to want to press clay when we feel it in our hands and to give some kind of form to it. This is also an ideal way to become familiar with the properties of different clays – some will be easier to handle than others and some will start to break or crack at an earlier stage. Pinching the clay in a controlled way allows you to make pots of quite varied shapes.

A pinch pot is created from a lump of clay simply by manipulating it into a smooth ball, then pushing your thumb into the center, and enlarging the hole by pinching the clay between your fingers.

1 Provide a firm support for the ball of clay by cupping one hand under the other. Then push into the center with your thumb to make a hollow. Start working the piece of clay around in your hand in a circular movement.

2 Continue to support the clay in the palm of your hand and enlarge the hollow by pinching the clay between your thumb and fingers. Do this until you have achieved an even pot shape.

coiling

Coiling is a wonderful means of exploring all sorts of shapes and forms. Coils have been used to create pots for thousands of years and the peoples of the ancient civilizations, such as those of South America, produced coiled pots of high quality and sophisticated design.

You can make coil pots as large as you like, but you must keep the clay fairly moist all the time so that the coils can be pushed and smoothed together easily. The coils should be of even size, about the width of a little finger. Remember that the diameter of each circle you add will determine if the pot is becoming wider or narrower as you increase its height. Keep checking visually as you add coils to maintain the shape of your pot.

2 Form the first coil on a pot by placing it on a circular base cut from an even slab of clay. Cut the slab on a banding wheel, if you have one, as the circular lines will allow you to cut a perfect circle. Push the coil down onto the slab with your thumb and, at the same time, pull the clay up on the outside with your first three fingers.

3 Add more coils, squeezing them together by pushing each one down with your thumb and up with your fingers. You may find it helpful to support the pot with your other hand.

1 If you need small coils, roll them in your hands, but roll longer coils on a table. Roll the coils of clay using the pads of your hands for even pressure. Keep your hands flat and roll from the center of the clay, gradually moving outward.

slabbing

Slabs of clay are a versatile way of constructing pots since they can be used to make flat pieces of any shape and also curved into cylinders. They can be cut to any required accurate size simply by measuring.

It is important to roll the slabs evenly so that each cut piece corresponds to the next. If possible, roll out a slab that is large enough to cut all the individual pieces from. For the best results, you will need a rolling pin, cloth and wooden battens to keep the clay an even width.

If you are joining two slab edges at right angles to each other, score the edges, then apply a little slip so that the pieces will adhere well together. To strengthen joints, say on a large rectangular pot such as a dish or tray, press a small clay coil over each corner both inside and outside the pot. This will help hold the slabs together and can also be embellished as an attractive decorative feature.

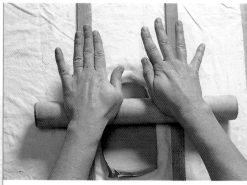

2 Roll the slab with the palms of both your hands on the rolling pin. This will help you exert an even pressure so that the slab is even.

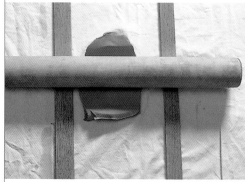

1 Place a piece of linen cloth or sheeting on the table. This will ensure a smooth surface for the slab of clay when it is rolled. Place a lump of clay between two battens of the same depth. The battens should be as far apart as the width that you want your rolled slab to be. Then start rolling the clay with a rolling pin.

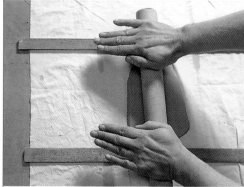

3 Turn the slab of clay and roll it in the opposite direction.

4 Peel the slab away from the cloth and turn it over. Then roll the other side in both directions to ensure that the slab is completely even and smooth.

5 To cut away ragged edges, use a wooden batten or straight edged rule and a sharp stiff knife.

(right) This decorative box is made from simple slabs. See page 94 for instructions on how to make it.

throwing

**Your early attempts to throw pots on the wheel will provide
you with a great deal of both fun and frustration.**

Learning to center the clay on the wheel is essential. Secure the clay in the middle of the wheel and use your arms and hands to push the clay into a balanced shape that does not wobble as you work on it. The wheel exerts a tremendous outward force and you must push against this. Once the clay is centered you can then start to open it up, making a bowl shape at first, then progressing to straight cylinders and vessels such as vases and jugs. The clay should be moist and it is helpful to keep a bowl of water nearby to keep your hands wet.

1 Make sure that the wheel is completely clean. Then place a moist ball of clay in the center. Start revolving the wheel and squeeze the clay at the bottom with the palms of your hands. Tuck your elbows in to your body so that you can exert more pressure through your hands and be in complete control.

2 Continue to squeeze the clay, guiding it up into a cone shape. Keep the wheel revolving fairly fast throughout the whole process of throwing.

3 With one hand still guiding the clay, use the other to push the cone down, flattening the top. This centering technique not only ensures that the clay is central on the wheel but also pushes out any odd air bubbles that might remain in the clay. Do this several times until the clay feels evenly balanced.

4 Start making an opening by pushing down with the flat tips of the first two fingers of one hand. Continue to support and guide the clay with the palm of the other hand.

6 Make a ridge in the bottom of the rim with your knuckle and push gently against the clay so that it rises upwards. Support the shape on the inside with the fingers of your other hand. Pull the clay up from the bottom to start increasing the height of the pot. Guide the clay into the shape you want as you draw it up.

8 Smooth the top of the pot, gently holding it between the thumb and fingers of one hand and resting the tip of the forefinger of the other hand on top while the wheel is revolving. Clean the base line of the pot by neatly trimming it with a wooden modeling tool.

5 Draw out the clay to make a base for the pot. Use both hands for this and be careful not to push down too hard or you may make the base too thin.

7 Strengthen the rim between the fingers of one hand, with the tip of the forefinger inside the pot. Guide the shape between the tips of the fingers and thumb of the other hand. A good rim helps to define the shape of the pot.

9 Remove the pot from the wheel by carefully cutting with a cheesewire. Clean any waste clay from the wheel so that it cannot harden and spoil the next pot you throw.

decorating

Decorating your pots gives you ample opportunity to put your own individual style on them. You can leave them as plain-colored clay and just add pattern to them by impressing or embossing, using sprigs or stamps. Or you can incise patterns with modeling tools or pieces of wood and add texture by gently pressing materials into the surface.

The whole world of color is also open to you. Colored slips can be used as all-over surface background, for trailing line patterns, or for spattering to give an attractive speckled effect. Or you can try out your painterly skills and apply pigments with a variety of brushes. Sketch out your design first to check that it will complement the shape of the pot.

applying **color**

Decorating is one of the most enjoyable stages in pottery and a plain pot can take on a completely different look when color is added.

Underglaze colors can be bought as powders and painted on with a brush, giving you ample opportunity for creative expression and fun. Add water to the powders to make a wash. The paint needs to be mixed well so that it is smooth with no lumps that might dry as hard particles and spoil the surface of your pot. Aim for a fairly rich mixture – one that is too watery will give an insipid effect.

Use a white china plate or piece of glass as a mixing palette so that you can see the colors properly, but remember that some colors change in firing so you need to try them out on a practice piece of clay first. Underglaze colors can be mixed together to modify and create new tones and you can even paint one color on top of another as long as it is not too thick. Glaze will not run over a thick surface of paint properly, giving an uneven finish.

It is best to use natural-hair brushes for painting as they have more spring, are easier to use, and give more life to your strokes. Oriental brushes are particularly useful; they produce

interesting marks and hold a good quantity of paint. Or you could try other paint techniques such as stamping using sponges, and stenciling.

A note of safety before you start painting – do not breathe in powders or put anything with paint on it into your mouth. Wash your hands well after using glaze colors. Many paints are toxic.

Underglaze powder paints are available in a wide range of colors.

Mix underglaze powder colors with water to make a smooth wash. Experiment with your colors because the final fired effect will probably look different from the color of the wash – for instance, cobalt blue looks mauve when you apply it as a wash. You can mix the colors as you would other paints to produce new colors.

texture **and decoration**

Look out for anything with a textured surface that can be used to produce an all-over texture on clay. Rough-woven fabrics are particularly useful for large areas and the surfaces of natural objects such as wood and seashells can enhance the surface of your pots when gently impressed into them.

All sorts of instruments can be used to make patterns as surface decoration. You can stamp into the clay to leave an impression of an object or incise a design with a sharp-pointed tool. Choose items that will leave a clean edge on the clay, so that the light can catch the finished pot and enhance the design with some shadow.

It is fun to make your own sprigging tools to produce embossed or impressed patterns. Whatever the design on the tool, the reverse effect will be produced as a sprig on the surface of the clay when you press the tool into it.

It is useful to make a number of sprigging tools to have on hand for decoration when you need them.

To make a sprigging tool, take a small ball of clay then roll it into the shape of a stamp, flattening the end. Use any item to impress a mark into it. Then fire the clay to make a permanent tool.

Sprigging tools can be whatever size or shape you wish to make them. Remember that the pattern will stamp out as the reverse of the tool, so an impressed design will give an embossed effect to the clay.

Many items can be used to stamp or impress marks, texture, and pattern into clay. Wood, plastic, and metal can all be pressed straight into the clay or used to make a sprigging tool.

using **slip**

If you are using a dark clay and wish to decorate on a light surface, then you will need to apply a coat of slip to the pot. Slip is simply a liquid mixture of powder clay thinned with water to the consistency of heavy cream. Push the mixture through a fine-meshed strainer (say, 120 mesh) to ensure that it is smooth.

You might choose to decorate your pots with colored slip. You can stir underglaze colors into the slip and then trail the liquid to make patterns on your pots using a slip bottle. If you are applying slip you should do this at the "green" stage of your pot, when the clay is soft to leather hard.

Of course, you can also apply colored glazes. These can now be bought ready mixed or you can make up mixtures to a wealth of recipes. See the chapter on Firing and Glazing, pages 34–43.

Ready-made slips are available in bottles or you can make your own by stirring in underglaze colors, making sure that you strain the mixture carefully to remove any lumps.

1 To make a slip, first take a scoop of dry slip powder and add it to a bucket.

2 Add water gradually and mix the slip with a stiff brush, trying to remove as many lumps as possible.

3 Continue to mix the slip into as smooth a liquid as possible. Pour it into a clean bucket through a strainer resting on battens and pushing through with a stiff brush.

4 Strain the slip mixture three or four times, changing to a strainer with a finer mesh each time and making sure you are pushing the slip into a clean bucket to avoid impurities.

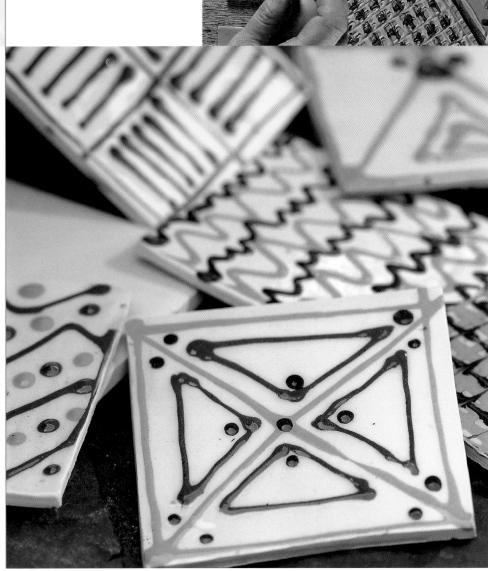

5 If you wish to make a colored slip, add underglaze powder colors or oxides, mixing with a brush until completely smooth. The slip should be the consistency of heavy cream.

(right and top right) These tiles are decorated with lines and dots of colored slip. See page 88 for instructions on how to make them.

firing
.and
glazing

To harden the clay and turn your work of art into a real pot it needs to be fired. The first firing, called biscuit firing, takes place after you have applied any colored slip and decoration. A further glaze firing is then necessary if you wish to apply a protective surface to your pot, whether glossy or matte.

Safety is of the utmost importance here, so remember you are dealing with potentially dangerous substances and equipment when firing and glazing. Mixing glazes correctly, applying them, and following the correct procedure when packing the kiln is essential – this firing stage is the most crucial time for the success of your pot. Your pottery supply store will answer any doubts and queries about temperatures required for different clays and glazes.

glazes **and glazing**

Glazing produces the protective surface that you apply to your pot. When heated at high temperature in a kiln, the ingredients in a glaze form an impervious glassy layer that makes the clay resistant to water. Glazes may be glossy or matte, translucent or opaque, whatever you prefer. They are applied prior to the final firing of a pot.

If you have applied colored slip or painted decoration to your pot, you will probably want to apply a clear glaze. If you wish to apply a colored glaze to a plain biscuited pot, however, an infinite variety of decorative effects and colors can be produced by the chemical reaction of oxides at high temperature. You can buy ready-prepared glazes for pottery from your pottery supply store. These are available in various colors and you simply apply them by brush. You can also make up your own glazes by mixing glaze ingredients to a recipe.

Before you apply a glaze, make sure that it will "fit" the clay you are using. Different firing temperatures are required for different glazes, which must also be suitable for the type of clay used. If the temperature, glaze, and clay are not all compatible the final surface may have flaws such as crazing (fine cracks in the surface).

Recipe for clear glaze suitable for earthenware

Lead bisilicate 68%
China clay 12%
Cornish stone 15%
Whiting 5%

Safe storage and use of glazes

Keep all materials in a safe place and keep the lids on containers so that they do not dry out. Make sure that all glaze containers are labeled accurately. Avoid inhaling glazes and do not allow children to put their fingers into liquid or unmixed glazes – always keep in mind that these are toxic substances.

preparing **glaze**

Whether you are following a recipe for a glaze or using a ready-prepared glaze available from a pottery supply store, you must make sure that the ingredients are well mixed. A smooth mixture will give a smooth finish to your pots.

When mixing glazes, wear an apron or protective clothing that can be washed. Wear a mask when weighing out dry compounds, and, to avoid handling them, use a scoop or plastic jug. You will need accurate weighing scales so that you can translate the percentages in recipes into the correct measures.

I Accurately weigh out the powders required to mix your glaze.

2 Mix all the dry material together in a large bucket.

3 Add water gradually – about half the amount of the dry ingredients.

4 Use your hand and arm or a piece of batten to mix the glaze up – you may wish to wear gloves. Try to break up any large lumps with your hands. Dig deep into the mixture to make sure all the colors are mixed together.

5 Keep mixing until the glaze is fairly smooth and there are only small lumps left.

6 Then place two battens over a clean bucket and ladle the glaze through a wide mesh strainer, say about 60 mesh. Push the mixture through the strainer with a glaze brush, a rubber kidney, or with your hands.

7 Ladle the mixture into a clean bucket using a finer (say, 100) mesh. Repeat this process two or three times using finer meshes so that you produce a smooth liquid the consistency of light cream.

8 Push any lumps through the strainer with a glaze brush, rubber kidney, or with your hands.

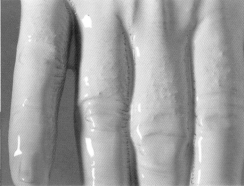

9 Use a rubber kidney to ensure that any last small lumps are smoothed out.

10 Test the consistency of the glaze by putting your hand in the bucket. If it is right you will see the little hairs on your hand – if it is too thick, the hairs will be covered.

applying **glaze**

Glaze should be applied evenly on your pot after it has been biscuit fired. If you are using a commercially made brush-on glaze, you must be careful not to overlap the edges when you apply it, otherwise the fired result may look uneven. Applying several thin coats may help to even out the layers. Many potters use a special large brush or glaze mop to apply glaze, and you may find this easier.

If you have a large enough quantity of glaze, the best way to apply it is by pouring and dipping. There is a special technique to this that is speedy and avoids applying the glaze too thickly. It may be necessary to stir the glaze first, especially if it has been standing for a while because sediment may settle at the bottom of the bucket.

Decide on the order of glazing inside and outside by the shape of your pot and whether it has a foot ring to hold on to or not. Always wipe off any drips of glaze from the bottom of a pot with a clean damp sponge – there must be no traces of glaze that might stick to the shelf in the kiln. As a precaution apply a coat of batt wash to the kiln shelves; this will serve as a protective coating for the shelf if the glaze runs a bit when fired.

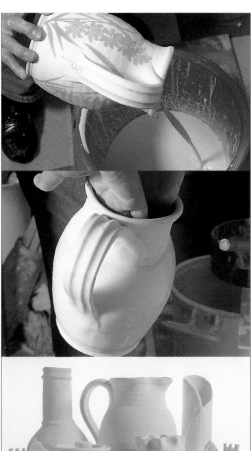

1 On a thrown object such as a bowl it is best to glaze the inside first. Do this by ladling or pouring the glaze into it and swirling it around. Then pour the glaze out over the rim by holding the foot of the pot, with the pot at an angle, and give it a little twist with your wrist.

2 Wait for the pot to dry a little. If you are glazing a cylindrical shape without a foot ring, such as a jug, plunge the pot upright into the glaze, flexing out your fingers inside it to grip the pot. Give the pot a little twist as you remove it from the glaze to loosen any drips. Remember to wipe off the bottom of the pot thoroughly with a damp sponge. If your pot has a foot ring, hold the pot upside down by its foot and plunge it into the glaze bucket up to the foot ring. Twist it gently as you remove it to shake off any drips.
If your fingers touch the glazed pot accidentally, or any parts get missed, you can finish them off with a brush.

3 Glazed pots ready for firing.

firing **and kilns**

Firing is the process by which the clay is hardened by extreme heat and becomes a functional pot. It necessitates the use of a kiln. Firing can be by oxidization, in which oxygen circulates freely in the kiln, or by reduction, in which the amount of oxygen is reduced. There are usually two firings for a pot – a biscuit firing and a glaze firing. It is wise always to biscuit fire your pot for added protection prior to glaze firing.

If a kiln is too expensive, or you simply do not have the space for one, do not despair. As usual, your pottery supply store may well solve the problem. They may be able to fire your pots themselves or know a potter who can. Failing that, your local art college may be able to help.

Choosing a kiln

There are several factors to take into account when selecting a kiln. Your budget will have some bearing, but so too will the amount of space you have available, the type of clay you wish to fire, and how you wish to fire it.

In a domestic situation, the most suitable kiln is probably powered by gas or electricity. Earthenware fires well in an electric kiln, but if you are producing stoneware pots you may prefer a gas-powered kiln so that you have more immediate control over the atmosphere for a large variety of glazes. Kilns are available as front or top loaders, and it is a matter of personal choice as to which you find most convenient.

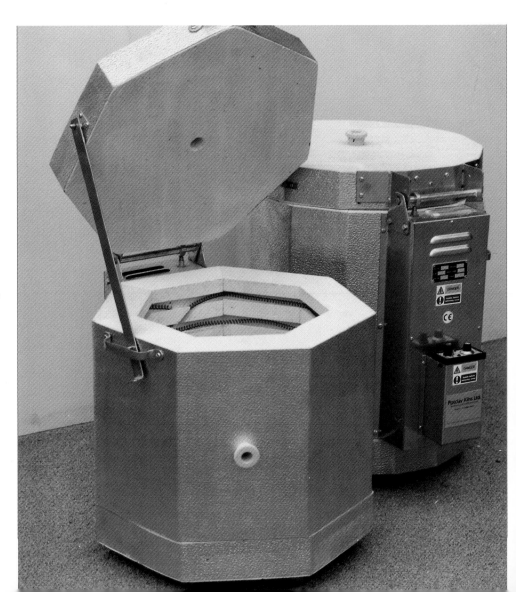

Kiln furniture

Inside the kiln you will need kiln shelves. Coat them in a glaze-resistant solution of batt wash to protect them. Props are used to support the shelves and these are available as interlocking shapes so that you can extend their height. If you have decorated both sides of a piece, use stilts to keep them clear of the shelves.

Specially made pyrometric cones are useful to check on the temperature inside the kiln. They are designed to stand on a small piece of clay and to melt and curve over when subjected to heat for a certain amount of time and when they reach the desired temperature.

(below) A selection of batts, interlocking extension props, castellated props, square props, stilts, and pyrometric cones. Choose kiln furniture that is appropriate for the shape and size of pots you are firing.

Once your kiln is installed, make sure that it has adequate ventilation; you do not want to inhale harmful fumes. Have an exhaust fan fitted if possible. While you are firing it may be appropriate to wear a mask as a safety precaution against any noxious fumes.

If you are buying an electric kiln, it is very useful to choose one that has a temperature gauge or pyrometer on the outside so that you know the temperature the kiln has reached; otherwise use pyrometric cones.

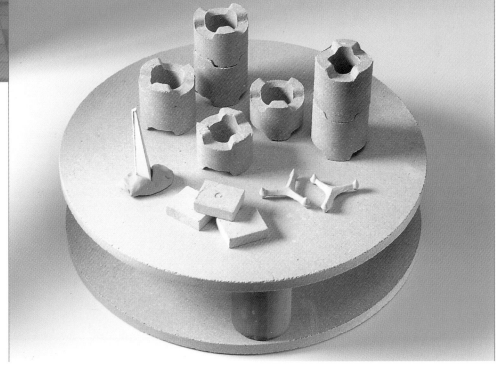

biscuit **firing**

A biscuit firing is always advisable because you can then glaze the pot later with less risk of damaging it. It hardens the clay "into pot," yet leaves the surface porous to accept the glaze.

Check that the pots have dried out enough to biscuit fire – clay lightens in color as it dries – and the pot is not cold to the touch.

At the biscuit firing, because there is no glaze that might run, you can pack quite a number of pots in the kiln. They can be placed so that they are touching or even inside or on top of one another as there is no likelihood of them sticking. Remember, however, that they are extremely fragile until they are "made" pots, so make sure you leave a good airflow around each piece.

Most clays are biscuit fired up to a temperature of 1796–2012°F (980–1100°C). When you are biscuit firing you should bring the temperature in the kiln up very slowly. The first stage of 32–932°F (0–500°C) is the trickiest. You need to allow roughly an hour in the kiln for each 212–302°F (100–150°C), so a complete biscuit firing will take about seven to 10 hours.

When the pots have been biscuited they can be left in a safe place for some time before further decoration or glazing as you wish.

Pots can be packed close together in the kiln for a biscuit firing, but make sure there is space around each for the air to circulate freely.

glaze firing

Glaze firing completes the making of your pot and it demands a great deal of care, both for yourself and your pot.

Remember that the kiln reaches very high temperatures and that toxic fumes can be given off during the firing process. If you are firing in your own kiln at home make sure that the room is properly ventilated. Wear a mask even to turn up the temperature of the kiln.

Packing the kiln for glaze firing takes a bit more thought than for biscuiting. Glazes can run, so it is important that the pots do not touch each other or they might stick. Place them on special kiln props if necessary.

Before firing the kiln, check on the temperature required. This needs to be suitable for both the clay you are using and the glaze you have applied. The process of firing will take about seven to nine hours and depends to some extent on the size of the kiln – a small kiln heats up to the required temperature more quickly than a large one. Make sure that nothing is placed on top of the kiln.

Check on the progress of the firing by looking through the spyhole at a safe distance. The pyrometer on the side of the kiln will indicate the temperature

reached, but for a foolproof method you should place pyrometric cones inside the kiln before you start to fire, securing them on a piece of clay. The cones will melt and curve right over when a specific temperature is reached.

The color of the pots will change from black to red black, to orange, to yellow, to white during firing. If you are firing to a temperature of, say, 2084°F (1140°C), then at around 2012°F (1100°C) observe through the spyhole to see if the cone is bending. If you look at the surface of a curved pot near the spyhole you will see a sheen on the pot when it is ready. Move your eye backward and forward to see the light catching the surface.

If the pot is not quite ready, hold the temperature by "soaking" the kiln using the pyrometer dial or switch or by turning the kiln back a bit. This process of maintaining the vitrification temperature can give the glaze a more mature appearance.

Switch off the kiln when the pots are ready and leave it to cool for 12 or more hours before opening it and removing the pots.

(left) Make sure that all glaze has been cleaned off the bottom of the pots before placing them in the kiln for glaze firing. Keep the pots apart to avoid sticking and place them on a batt coated with batt wash so that any glaze that runs can be chipped off afterward.

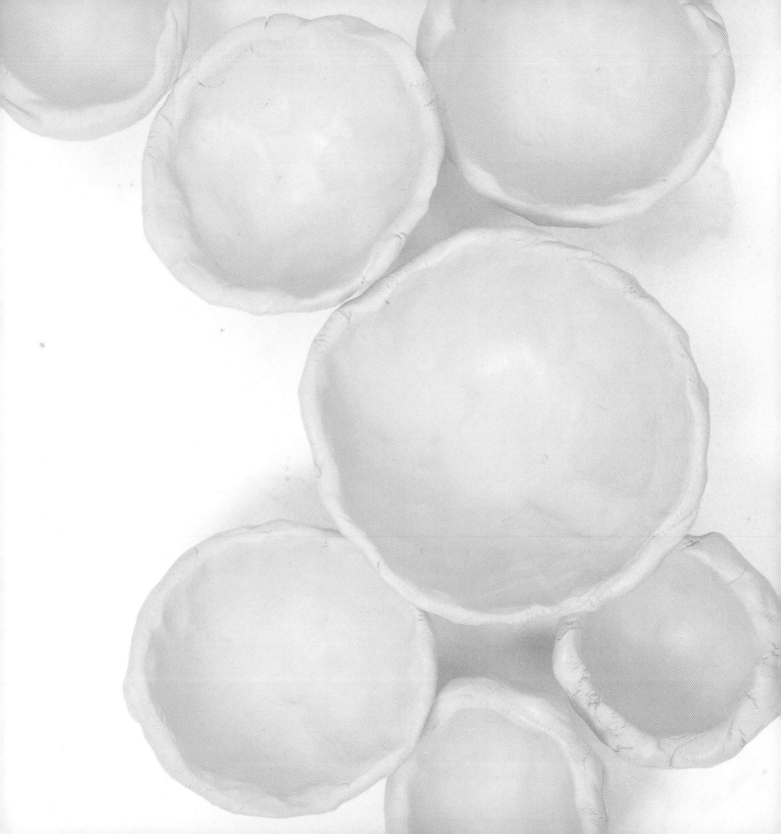

pinch
pots

Just by pinching clay into shape you can make all sorts of pots. The pinch pot projects shown here are made from small balls of clay that are easy to work with. The decoration enhances or balances the shape of the hand-molded clay, and you could try your own versions of the same pot. For instance, instead of making a pomander embossed with sprigs of lavender you might produce a design with a variety of herbs. Children will love the ocarina (hand flute), which can be decorated in as many bright colors as you wish. The buttons and beads are an ideal way of trying out textures and patterns, and the sculpted pebbles take the ideas a bit further by joining two pots to make a new natural-looking form.

pomander

Here is a simple pinch-pot pomander to start you off. The pomander is decorated with painted lavender sprigs and would make an ideal gift filled with sweet-smelling dried lavender. If you prefer a more exotic look, you could paint it in oranges and reds and fill it with a spicy potpourri.

tools and equipment

Potter's knife

Small natural sponge

Hole cutter

Toothbrush

Sprigging tool

Metal kidney

1 Make a hollow pinch pot (see Basic Techniques, on pages 20–27). Scrape the surface with a metal kidney so that it is smooth, working the clay into a ball shape.

2 Roll the ball of clay to give a good finish to the surface and even out the shape.

3 Use a sprigging tool or stamp to make an embossed design for the pomander. You can make your own by taking an impression of lavender in a piece of clay and biscuit firing it (see Decorating, on pages 28–33). Push a small roll of clay into the sprigging tool, flattening it down. When you remove it you will have an embossed decoration to apply.

4 Moisten the side of the pomander and roughen the surface of the clay a little with an old toothbrush. This provides a key so that the decoration can adhere to the pot. Then add the pieces of embossed clay around the outside of the pomander.

5 Cut holes in the top of the pomander so that the scent of the lavender or potpourri can escape.

6 Cut a small disk of clay and place it on the top of the pomander in the center of the holes. Impress a sprig decoration on it.

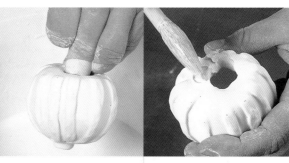

10 Paint the top decoration of the pomander in the same colors to hold the design together.

11 Dip the painted pomander in glaze, holding it by curling your finger inside through the hole. Gently shake off any drips of glaze.

12 Touch up any areas of missed glaze with a brush.

13 After firing, the pomander can be filled with lavender. Plug the hole in the base with cork.

8 Paint decoration on the pomander after biscuit firing. Put lavender blue onto the petals of each of the lavender sprigs.

7 This shows the finished pomander and another one in the making. The pomander is filled through the hole in the base, which can be plugged later by a piece of cork. Leave the clay to dry before biscuit firing the pots.

9 Now paint green spiked leaves on the flat areas in between the lavender sprigs.

ocarina

An ocarina is a small hand flute that is fun to make and with a bit of luck you might also be able to get a tune out of it. Its name refers to its shape (Italian oca meaning goose's egg). This simplified version has only three finger holes, but you could put in more if you wish.

1 Roll out a slab of clay (see Basic Techniques, on pages 20–27) and cut a circular disk about 5 inches in diameter from it using a cardboard template. Fold over the disk so that the edges meet.

2 Pinch the edges together with your thumb and forefinger.

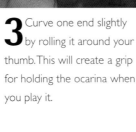

3 Curve one end slightly by rolling it around your thumb. This will create a grip for holding the ocarina when you play it.

4 Using a knife, cut a scoop for the mouthpiece in the center of the rounded edge.

5 Pinch around the mouthpiece so that its edges are thin. Then smooth them off by rubbing with your fingers over a piece of sheeting and use the same method to smooth the joints of the ocarina. Blow into the ocarina through the mouthpiece to enlarge the shape if necessary. Leave the ocarina to dry slightly.

6 When the clay is leather hard, cut three or four finger holes on one side using a hole cutter. These need to be cleanly cut. Place them where they will be comfortable for playing the instrument.

9 Then trail lines of brown slip on both halves, three on one side and two shorter ones on the other so that the design does not look too symmetrical. Be careful not to block the finger holes with the slip.

10 Finish the decoration with some dots of green slip. Wipe off any unwanted decoration with a damp sponge. Then biscuit fire the ocarina.

11 Finally, glaze and fire the ocarina and try playing it!

8 Repeat the yellow lines on the other half.

7 Using yellow slip in a slip bottle, trail four lines of decoration on one half of the playing side.

buttons and beads

Here is a simple idea that has maximum impact and provides endless possibilities for decoration. Give clothes a personal touch by making your own patterned buttons and complete your accessories with rows of beautiful textured clay beads.

1 Make your own patterned sprigging tools (see Decorating, on pages 28–33). To make a button, take a small, even ball of clay and simply push the tool into it, flattening the back in the palm of your hand as you do so. The sprigging tool will leave a clear embossed impression.

2 Make two thread holes in the button by gently pushing the end of a paintbrush through the clay.

3 It is easy to make round beads simply by pushing the end of a paintbrush through a tiny ball of clay. For rectangular beads, put a lump of clay on the end of a brush and flatten to give it four sides. You may find a metal kidney useful for this. Press a sprigging tool onto all four sides for a textured surface. Remove the paintbrush carefully.

4 Lay the buttons and beads out in rows to dry before decorating.

5 The unglazed buttons are fired in a glaze firing.

sculpted pebbles

***T**hese sculpted pebbles have advantages over real stones as they can be custom-made to suit the colors, shapes, and sizes you require for any decorative use indoors and out. They are ideal for creating a small Japanese-style garden or bonsai arrangement.*

tools and equipment

Large pebble

Textured piece of wood

Corrugated cardboard

Potter's knife

Small natural sponge

Slip bottle

Toothbrush

Film canister

1 The pebbles are made by joining two pinch pots together (see Basic Techniques, on pages 20–27). This photograph shows the progress of a ball of clay to pinch pot.

2 Hold a ball of clay firmly in the palm of your hand. Push in the thumb of your other hand and start shaping a hollow as you work the clay around.

3 Create a bowl shape by pinching with your thumb and fingers as you rotate the clay.

4 Make a second bowl shape. If necessary, before joining the two shapes, fill the center with paper to give form to the pebble you are making.

5 Start joining the two bowl shapes together. For this pebble no paper support is needed.

6 Pinch firmly across the seam to join the two pieces. Push the pebble into shape. Make a hole in the top of the pebble so that air can escape when the clay is later fired in the kiln. If you have used paper as a support inside, remove it at this stage, pulling it out through the hole. Then make as many more pebbles as you wish.

7 There are many ways of decorating pebbles. Here, a natural stone is used to impress texture. Rotate the pebble carefully so that the texture is evenly applied over every surface.

9 Corrugated cardboard makes an unusual texture. Apply it horizontally across the pebble holding it at a slight angle.

11 Dip the toothbrush into the slip and run your fingers across the bristles, directing the slip to the top of the pebble. This can be a messy job, so make sure you have plenty of space around you. Then dip the toothbrush into the slip again and apply it to the bottom of the pebble.

12 Leave the pebbles to dry before firing. When you put the pebbles in the kiln for firing, make sure that the holes are upright so that air can escape and the pebbles will not explode.

13 (below) The biscuited pebbles are finished with a coat of boot polish and beeswax and can be used in an attractive bonsai arrangement.

8 You can use ridged or textured wood to make an attractive surface pattern on the pebbles.

10 Colored slip spattered with an old toothbrush looks effective. An empty film canister makes a useful container for the slip.

coil
pots

One of the advantages of making pots from coils is that you can produce many different forms, including sculptural ones, that are not possible on the wheel. To start you off, here are some ideas for manageable coiled pots – a bottle vase, serving bowl, and votive candle holders.

Take your time, and keep the clay moist so that it can be manipulated with ease, because you need to control the shaping of the pot as you work up its height. It may take some practice to achieve the exact shape you want and to get the pot even, but do not worry if the final result is not as you planned – handmade pieces are not expected to look perfectly symmetrical and a bit of character adds to the charm.

bottle **vase**

The slim neck of this coiled bottle vase is defined by adding rings, and the sides are flattened by paddling. Make the vase as big or small as you like. Break each coil off as you complete the circle, and stagger the joints for a sturdy, even pot.

tools and equipment

Banding wheel (or cake turntable)

Small natural sponge

Throwing hook

Potter's knife

Wooden modeling tool

Metal kidney

Throwing rib (or old credit card)

Serrated metal modeling tool

1 Use moist clay to avoid cracking – coiling is a slow process and drying out must be prevented. Place a slab of clay on the banding wheel and cut a disk from it. Start coiling around the base, pushing down with your thumb inside the pot and pushing the clay up on the outside with three fingers of the same hand (see Basic Techniques, on pages 20–27). Continue to add coils, holding the coil up and joining it as you work so that you can control the shape of the pot.

2 After every three coils, smooth them together with your forefinger. This also helps you check the shape of the pot. For this bottle vase it is necessary to create a slightly bellied-out shape. To do this, place the next coil on the outside lip of the pot, angling your hands slightly outward.

3 When you have smoothed the coils together with your finger, smooth the surface of the clay with a metal kidney. Sweep up and around with the kidney, concentrating on the shape you are making. Pat down any rough clay. Also smooth the inside of the pot as you go or it will become difficult for you to reach the inside.

4 If the shape of the pot becomes uneven, correct it by adding a fatter or thinner coil as necessary. Continue smoothing the clay with your finger and the metal kidney after every three coils. Join the top two coils and then the bottom two rather than smoothing them all together because this will create a neater finish.

5 When the pot is about 4 inches high, start to shape inward by placing the coils on the inside edge and pushing outward. When the diameter of the top measures about 1½ inches, start to build straight upward, placing the coils evenly on top of one another to make the neck of the vase. Correct any uneven edges with a knife.

6 Smooth the sides of the neck with an old credit card. Then form a lip at the top of the neck by placing a wooden tool under the top coil and sweeping it horizontally around the pot. Add a further coil as decoration just below the lip to define the top of the pot. Pinch it between your finger and thumb to give a sharper outline. Smooth with a damp sponge.

7 Add another coil around the bottom of the neck of the vase.

8 Facet the sides of the body of the pot by paddling it with a flat-sided implement. You could also use a ruler, the back of a wooden spoon, a spatula, or a similar flat piece of wood. Tap the pot gently, working all around it, and increase the pressure gradually to make the size and shape of facet you require.

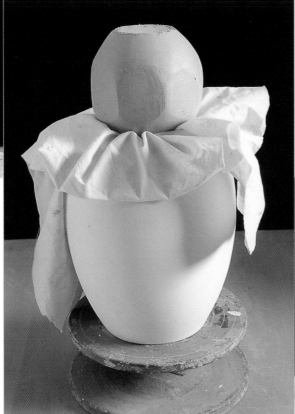

9 Look carefully at your pot when you have finished shaping it. In this case the vase needs a foot to "lift" the piece visually.

10 Place the pot upside down in another pot to support it. Put a piece of cloth inside the supporting pot first to protect the surface of the bottle vase.

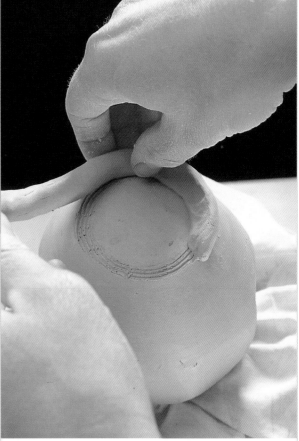

11 Use a serrated metal modeling tool to score a circle where the foot will be placed. This roughens the clay and provides a key so that the foot coil can adhere. Then add a coil, pushing firmly and smoothing inside the ring.

12 Correct the shape of the foot with an old credit card and smooth it with a piece of sheeting. Then carefully remove the vase from its supporting pot.

13 Leave the pot to dry before biscuit firing it.

14 Enhance the facets on the body of the pot by loosely painting blossoms in cobalt blue underglaze color. Paint an outline to resemble medallions.

15 Paint above and below the decorative coils on the neck and around the foot of the pot to emphasize these features. Paint vertical lines down the neck of the vase.

16 Paint the background of the body of the vase and, finally, paint around the top lip.

17 To glaze the vase hold it carefully by the lip and plunge the body of the pot into the bucket of glaze.

18 As you remove the vase from the glaze, give it a little twist to shake off any drips. Wipe the base of the pot with a damp sponge to remove glaze from under the foot ring. Leave to dry for a minute or two.

19 Glaze the inside of the vase by pouring glaze in, swirling it around, and then pouring it out at an angle, again giving the pot a little twist with your wrist.

20 Hold the pot by the foot ring and plunge it into the bucket of glaze to glaze the neck. Shake and twist it gently to loosen any drips as you remove it.

21 The fired pot has a distinct Asian style and elegance.

serving bowl

Traditional earthy colors inspired by a simple impressed decoration made with just a piece of wood give this serving bowl a rustic look. Use it for outdoor meals on summer evenings, for serving rice, pasta, or salad, or for informal winter suppers with family and friends.

tools and equipment

Potter's knife

Banding wheel (or cake turntable)

Linen or cotton sheeting

Battens

Rolling pin

Chamois

Rubber kidney

Metal kidney

Serrated metal modeling tool

1 Roll a slab of clay and cut a circular base from it on the banding wheel to measure 6 inches in diameter. Start the first coil, securing it on the inside of the base by firmly pushing the clay down with your fingers (see Basic Techniques, on pages 20–27).

2 Start adding further coils, pushing and pinching them together.

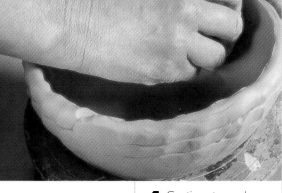

3 Smooth the edge of the pot with a metal kidney, then add further coils to open up the bowl shape. Make sure the coils are of equal thickness all the way around so that the pot keeps an even shape.

4 Continue to work on the inside of the pot with a metal kidney to maintain the shape.

5 Smooth inside the bowl with a rubber kidney for a neater finish.

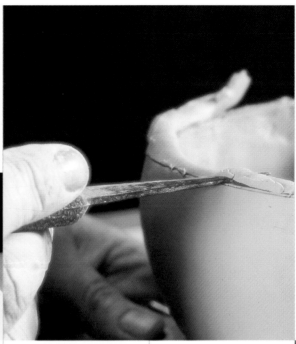

6 Smooth the outside of the bowl with the tip of your forefinger. Keep the pot steady by using your other hand as a guide inside.

7 Continue to refine the surface of the clay with a metal kidney, sweeping it around the shape of the outside of the bowl.

8 Even the top of the bowl by cutting it level with a knife, keeping the banding wheel revolving.

9 Smooth the rim of the bowl with the tips of your fingers over a piece of sheeting. Then finish off with a moist chamois.

10 From a slab of clay, cut two wedge shapes for the handles. Use a serrated metal modeling tool to score the surface of the bowl on each side where the handles are to be positioned.

11 Score down the edge of each handle and apply slip. Then push each handle carefully into position on the bowl.

14 Draw a line around the rim of the bowl by gently impressing the edge of a piece of wood into the clay.

15 The finished decoration on the bowl should look like a row of tepees.

13 Decorate the band further by impressing the edge of a smooth piece of wood into the clay to make angled lines. Make all the lines in one direction first, then do those in the opposite direction so that the pattern is consistent.

12 Use a rough-sawn piece of wood to impress a band of texture around the bowl.

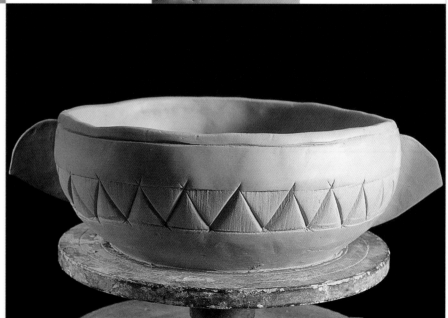

16 Leave the bowl out to dry before biscuit firing it.

17 Paint in the bottom triangles on the outside of the bowl using underglaze colors, alternating green and brown. Then paint all the top triangles in yellow.

22 Swirl the glaze inside the bowl, then pour off at an angle. Any missed areas can be finished off with a brush.

21 Glaze the outside of the bowl by plunging it. Shake off any drips and wipe off the bottom of the bowl with a damp sponge. Leave to dry for a minute or so, then ladle glaze into the inside of the bowl.

23 The glazed bowl ready for firing.

24 The glossy finish on the pot enhances the strong shapes of the decoration.

19 Paint the rim brown, then add a further line just beneath and under the triangles. Paint yellow, green, and brown circles of varying widths inside the bottom of the pot to finish.

18 Paint the side of the handles in green.

20 The decorated bowl is now ready for glazing.

votive **candle holder**

A votive candle holder casts a soft warm glow and adds atmosphere to any evening gathering. The shape of this starry holder was inspired by the form of a dried poppy head. For safety, never leave a candle unattended and make sure that it is out of reach of small children.

tools and equipment

Potter's knife

Banding wheel (or cake turntable)

Linen or cotton sheeting

Battens

Rolling pin

Throwing rib

Rubber kidney

Metal kidney

Hole cutter

Shape cutter

Serrated metal modeling tool

1 Roll a slab of clay and cut a circular base from it on the banding wheel to measure 3½ inches in diameter. Add the first coil, pushing the clay down firmly with your fingers so that it is secure on the inside of the base (see Basic Techniques, on pages 20–27). Add more coils and smooth inside with a rubber kidney as you go since you are making a closed space and it will be difficult to reach inside later.

2 As you add the coils, start taking the shape inward. Keep the clay moist to avoid cracking. Smooth the coils on the outside of the pot with the tip of your forefinger, using the other hand inside the pot to guide the shape.

3 Continue to add coils, narrowing the diameter of the pot at the top and smoothing them all the way round with your fingers.

4 Carefully use a metal kidney to remove any bumps from the surface of the clay and generally smooth it.

5 Continue to smooth inside the pot with a throwing rib.

6 Finish off the surface at the top of the pot by rubbing with your fingers over a piece of sheeting.

8 This shows the finished star-shaped top.

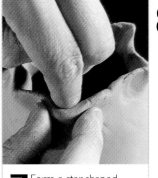

7 Form a star-shaped fluted top to the pot. Do this by placing the knuckle of your forefinger inside the pot and pinching against it on the outside with the finger and thumb of the other hand.

9 Pierce holes around the top of the candle holder with a hole cutter. You could also use a thick plastic drinking straw for a clean cut. Then mark the star shapes on the clay with a shape cutter. Do not cut out the star shapes yet because the clay is too soft and needs to dry a bit.

10 Place the candle holder upside down in another pot, protected by a cloth. Then score a circle with a serrated metal modeling tool where the foot ring will be added.

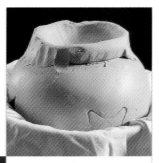

11 Add a coil to the bottom of the pot to make a foot ring and carefully push it onto the pot. Smooth it with your fingers, correcting the shape as you work.

12 Smooth inside the foot ring, then smooth outside with a metal kidney so that the clay has no visible joint.

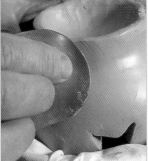

13 Finish the surface by smoothing inside and outside the foot ring with a rubber kidney.

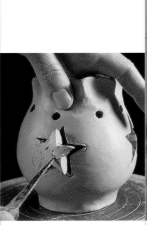

19 Outline the foot ring and the yellow rim in black and the decoration is finished.

14 Now that the clay is drier, cut around the star shapes with a knife.

15 Remove the star shapes by stabbing a knife into the center and lifting them out of the clay.

17 Paint inside the candle holder in blue. Then paint half the outside of the pot first. Pencil small circles for small stars on the outside of the pot. Paint these in yellow. Then paint the rim of the pot and the inner edges of the cut-out stars in yellow. Paint half the body of the pot in blue and outline the stars in black.

20 To glaze the candle holder, hold the pot by the foot and dip it into the glaze.

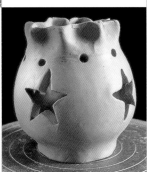

16 Leave the pot to dry before you start the biscuit firing.

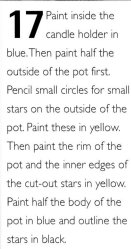

18 Complete the painting of the other half of the pot.

21 As the candle holder has holes in it, the inside is also glazed when you dip the pot.

22 Use a brush to dab glaze onto any missed areas.

slab
pots

Slabs of clay are often used to make a base for a coil or pinch pot, but they are used on their own when rectangular shapes are required. Simple straight-edged shapes can be used to make attractive items such as tiles, boxes, and frames. Sometimes it is helpful to use a former to mold the clay, and the platter and soapdish projects show you how to do this so that the clay falls naturally into shape.

Use slabs for large curved areas such as bookends, or wrap them into a tube or cylinder to make rainbow chimes and vases. Children particularly enjoy cutting out shapes and there are ideas here for tree decorations, checkers, and a mobile. The unusual chess pieces are made by wrapping small slab shapes into a cone and adding cut-out tops.

molded **platter**

By molding clay on formers you can produce dishes of uniform size. It is easy to make a former by biscuiting a slab of clay with a handle. The molded platter here is decorated by sponging on colored slip and then outlining the pattern with a trail of slip.

tools and equipment

Linen or cotton sheeting

Battens

Rolling pin

Potter's knife

Large clay former

Colored slips (green and black)

Slip bottle

Sponge pad

Small natural sponge

Paintbrushes

1 Roll out a slab of clay on a piece of cloth (see Basic Techniques, on pages 20–27) and place a former on top. The former used here is made from a fired slab of clay with a handle but you could use a well-sanded piece of wood or any kitchen bowl.

3 Use the cloth and a batten to push up the clay border against the former to make the sides of the platter. Do this for all four sides of the platter.

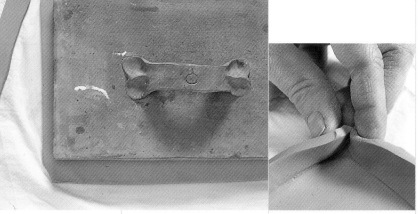

2 Cut around the former, leaving a border that you can fold up to make the edge of the platter.

4 Pinch the corners together so that the sides are firmly joined to one another.

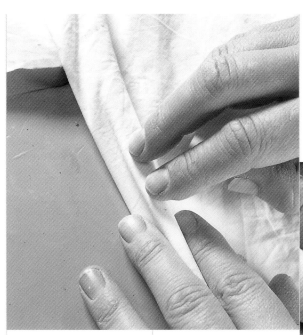

5 Smooth the cut edges of the clay by gently rubbing with your fingertips over a piece of sheeting. Similarly smooth the sides between your fingers.

6 Cut four small wedge-shaped slabs of clay. Place these in the corners of the platter.

7 Curve the top parts of the triangles over the tops of the curves. Push the wedges into the corners of the platter with the end of a piece of batten to make sure that they are secure.

8 With the side of the batten make decorative indentations. These decorative wedges serve both to strengthen the corners and to hide the joints in the clay.

9 Apply a thick layer of green colored slip with a brush to a sponge pad. You can use a kitchen sponge or made your own sponge stamp shapes. Press the sponge pad onto the dish to make a pattern with the colored slip. The dish here has three squares and you need to brush green slip onto the sponge for each application to make sure you achieve an even effect.

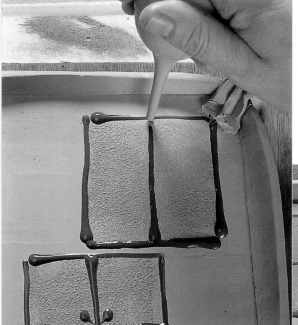

10 Fill a slip bottle with black slip and shake it gently to dispel any air bubbles. Make sure that the tip of the bottle is filled with liquid. Check that the slip is the right consistency by making a practice trail on a spare piece of paper. Then trail an outline around the green squares on the dish. Trail lines to divide the squares into four and make a small dot at the inner corner of each small square.

11 Use the tip of a small artist's brush to draw out slip from the centers of the black dots.

12 Trail lines of black slip around the sides of the dish to frame the design. Leave to dry before biscuit firing the platter.

13 Apply glaze to the dish by ladling it in, then pouring it off to ensure an even layer.

14 The finished dish after glazing is stylish enough to use on any dinner table.

soap dish

Paint this combined soap dish and toothbrush holder in bright or pastel colors to match your bathroom towels and accessories. Made by molding around a small former, the dish could be made without the additional ring as an attractive gift tray to hold candies or trinkets.

tools and equipment

Linen or cotton sheeting

Battens

Rolling pin

Potter's knife

Small wooden former

Block of wood

Hole cutter

Small natural sponge

1 Roll out a slab of clay (see Basic Techniques, on pages 20–27). Cut around a small wooden former, leaving an overlap all the way around. Then place the former on a wooden block and position the clay slab centrally on top.

3 The edges of the clay fall naturally over the former to create the shape of the dish. Make sure that the base of the dish is even. Leave the dish to dry a little before adding feet.

2 Use a rolling pin to strike the base of the block to settle the clay.

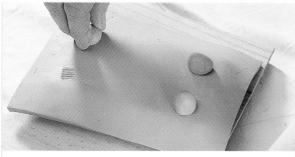

4 Scratch the base of the dish at the four points where the feet are to be added. Then attach small balls of clay to these scratched areas. To make the feet firm and as a decorative feature, press down each side of the balls of clay with the end of a piece of batten.

6 Scratch the surface of the soap dish where you wish to position the toothbrush holder and firmly press the ring onto the dish.

5 Cut a strip from a slab of clay and wrap it into a cylinder shape. Push on the joint to flatten it slightly and smooth it with your fingers or use a piece of wood. When the clay has dried a little, cut two holes with a hole cutter. Widen them with a knife so that they will hold toothbrushes.

7 The toothbrush holder is positioned at the end of the dish so that there is room for the soap (or toothpaste, if you prefer!).

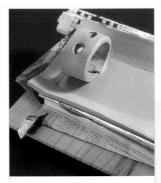

8 Leave the dish to dry before biscuit firing. Make a support for the clay with folded newspaper so that the sides will not sag.

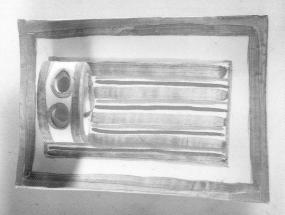

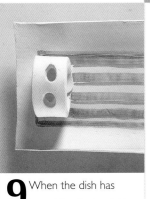

9 When the dish has been biscuited, paint in stripes in the center part. Here red stripes are outlined and framed with thinner blue stripes.

10 Paint in red and blue stripes on the toothbrush holder and around the edges of the dish. Add green stripes to the center part.

11 The finished decoration. Oriental brushes hold a good amount of paint and produce a flowing line.

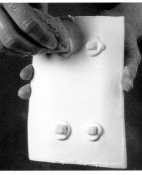

12 Dip the dish in a bucket of glaze.

13 Remove glaze from the base of the feet with a damp sponge. This is to prevent the dish from sticking to the kiln during glaze firing.

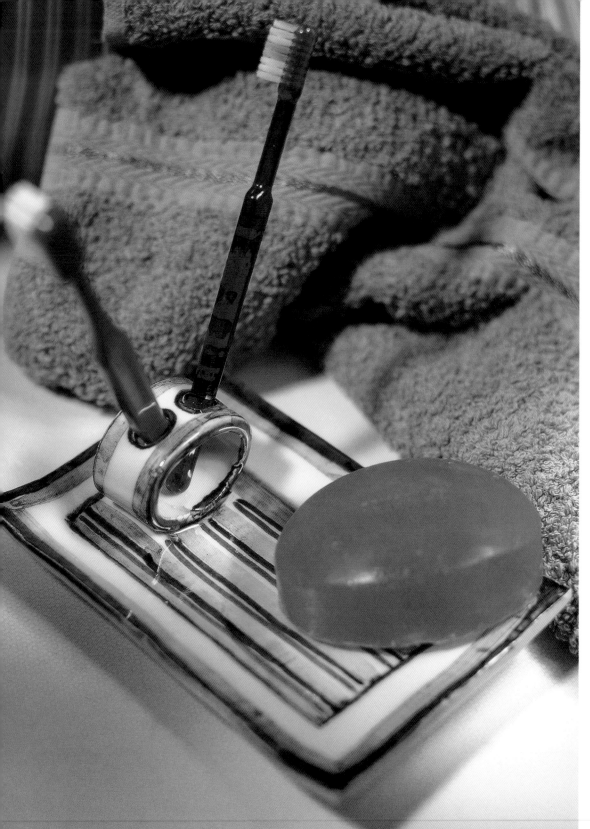

14 The bright, stripey soap dish makes a useful and colorful addition to a bathroom.

tree decorations

Indoor tree decorations are a simple way of adding a personal touch to any festive occasion. You can use shapes that are suitable for special events, parties, or anniversaries, and appropriate for individual friends and family. These decorations make unusual and attractive small gifts.

tools and equipment

Linen or cotton sheeting

Battens

Rolling pin

Potter's knife

Hole cutter

Small natural sponge

Shape cutters

Sprigging tools, embossed buttons, etc

1 Roll out a slab of clay (see Basic Techniques, on pages 20–27), then leave the clay to settle for a while.

2 Use shape cutters to cut cleanly through the moist clay. You may also wish to improvise and make your own cutters – a film canister with the end cut off makes a useful small round shape that you can push the clay through.

3 Decorate the shapes with sprigs. Press the sprigging tools directly into the clay, or make impressions on small flattened balls of clay, scoring slightly on the back and on the cut shape, and adding a little slip so that the pieces adhere. Cut a hole at the top of each shape with a hole cutter for hanging.

4 Leave the decorations to dry on a flat wooden board to help prevent them from warping.

5 The unglazed decorations are fired in a glaze firing. They look attractive added to an arrangement of winter twigs in a vase.

rainbow chimes

These rainbow-colored chimes are easy to make and assemble. Place them near an open window or door where they will tinkle in the breeze and provide a soothing background sound. You could also make them in terracotta clay for a more rustic look.

tools and **equipment**

Linen or cotton sheeting

Battens

Rolling pin

Circular template

Potter's knife

Hole cutter

Waxed string

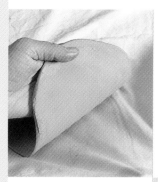

1 Roll out a slab of clay on a piece of linen sheeting (see Basic Techniques, on pages 20–27). Turn the slab over backward and forward on the sheeting to smooth the surface on both sides.

3 Make each chime separately. Wrap the strip of clay around the dowel and pinch the edges together. Make sure that you do not have excess clay on the joint or the air channel of the chime may become obstructed.

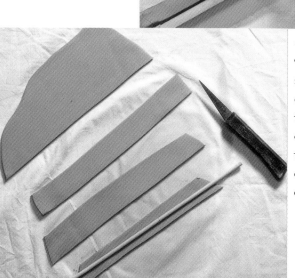

2 Cut strips of clay wide enough to go around a ¼-inch piece of wooden dowel about 12 inches long, allowing an overlap for joining. You will need four pairs of strips graduating down in length to make eight chimes. Cut a short strip, about 3 inches long, to make a "sail" that will hang down from the center to encourage the wind chimes to move.

4 Roll the tube of clay on sheeting to smooth the joint. This also helps loosen the clay from the wood.

6 Impress a line pattern on the cut end by rolling the tube under a thin piece of wood about ¾ inch from the end. Slide the cut piece off the dowel. Then slide the wood out of the tube and leave the clay to dry to leather hard.

5 Roll one end of the clay tube under a knife to cut a clean edge. Leave the other end as an overlap.

7 To make the central disk that the chimes will hang from, roll out a slab of clay and cut around a cardboard template about 3½ inches in diameter. Cut a small disk about 1 inch in diameter for the clapper or "sail." Leave both pieces to dry until the clay is leather hard.

8 When the central disk is leather hard, cut hanging holes around the edge with a hole cutter. Cut one hole in the middle for the disk to hang from. Cut another hole in the middle of the clapper.

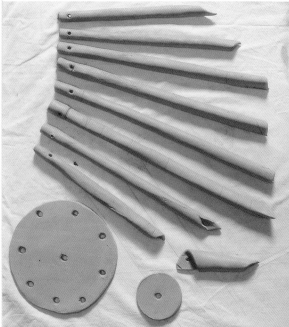

9 Make any pattern on the tubes when they are leather hard. Cut out holes to go right through the top of each tube and at the top of the small sail.

10 Lay the pieces out to dry before biscuit firing.

11 Use brush-on glazes in rainbow colors to decorate the chimes. Prop the chimes on star stilts in the kiln so that they will not touch and stick to the kiln shelves or to any other pots.

12 Use waxed string to assemble the chimes and place them near a window or doorway.

mobile

A mobile of butterflies and birds fluttering under a cloud from which peeps a rainbow will appeal to children of all ages. The very young will thoroughly enjoy this project, which is easy and fun to make. You can design a mobile around any theme, so make the most of your imagination.

tools and equipment

Linen or cotton sheeting

Battens

Rolling pin

Templates

Potter's knife

Shape cutters

Wooden modeling tool

Artist's brush

Waxed string

1 Make a cardboard template for the top part of the mobile. You may need to sketch out one or two versions on paper first to see how your design will look. Then roll out a slab of clay (see Basic Techniques, on pages 20–27) and turn it over on the sheeting to smooth it down on both sides. Place the cardboard template on top and cut carefully around the outline to give a clean edge.

2 Roll out a second slab of clay, remembering to turn it over on the sheeting so that you can smooth both sides with your fingers. Use shape cutters to cut out birds and butterflies or whatever hanging shapes you choose for your theme.

3 Clean any rough edges and bumps by cutting away with a knife. You can also outline the shape with a knife to give it sharp definition.

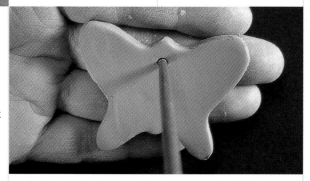

4 Use the end of a paintbrush to pierce holes for hanging the shapes. Make a hole at the top and the bottom of the shapes so that they can be threaded together. The bottom shape in a series needs a hole only at the top.

5 Add detail to the shapes if you wish. Here, the fantail of a dove is given more texture by making indentations in the clay with the end of a wooden modeling tool. Then make a small hole to indicate the eye of the bird.

6 Leave the pieces to dry on a wooden board before biscuit firing.

7 After painting and glazing, assemble the mobile with waxed string.

tiles

Handmade decorative tiles have an appeal and charm that is quite unique. These are all decorated by trailing colored slip, but you can paint a design on them or try any of the impressed or embossed effects described in other projects. Experiment with colors and patterns.

tools and equipment

Linen or cotton sheeting

Battens

Rolling pin

Potter's knife

Dentist's tool

Small natural sponge

Colored slips (yellow, green, and brown)

Slip bottles

Paintbrush or feather

1 Roll out a slab of clay (see Basic Techniques, on pages 20–27). Cut out exact squares for your tiles. Do this by marking the measurement on a batten and cutting against it up to the mark. Measure and cut several tile slabs.

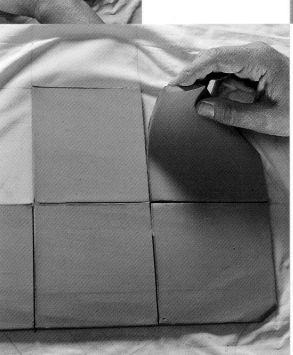

2 Peel the slabs off the sheeting. Cut off any bumps with a knife and clean the edges by smoothing between your fingers over the sheeting. Turn the tiles over and check the other side.

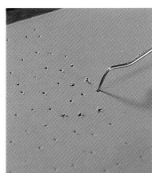

3 Prick the backs of the tiles with a dentist's tool or a fork or darning needle. This should prevent them from warping too much and aids the drying process. (Commercial tiles are made with ridges to allow air to circulate in the production process.)

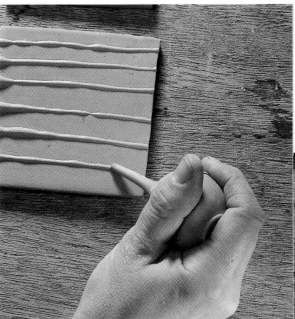

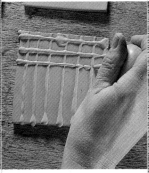

4 Start decorating the first tile. Fill the slip bottle with yellow slip and give it a little shake to dispel any air bubbles. Make sure that the tip of the bottle is filled with liquid. Test that the slip is the correct consistency by trying out a trail on a piece of board. Then trail lines of slip across the surface of the tile.

5 Pull lines across the tile at right angles to the first ones.

7 Draw the lines together in both directions with the end of a paintbrush. You may prefer to use the traditional method of using a feather for this—hence the term "feathering" for this traditional effect.

6 Fill another slip bottle with brown slip, shake, and test as before. Put a dot of slip in each of the squares.

8 On another tile, trail a zigzag line using green slip, remembering to test the consistency of the slip.

10 On a third tile, trail brown slip lines to divide it into four squares. Fill in one of the squares with small lines.

13 Add brown dots to the tops of the small triangles. Add brown dots to the center of the tile and corners of the large triangles to complete the decoration of the fourth tile.

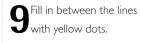

9 Fill in between the lines with yellow dots.

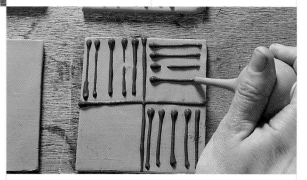

11 Complete the opposite corner square in the same way, then decorate the other two squares with lines pulled in the opposite direction.

12 For the fourth tile, trail yellow slip lines to divide it into four triangles. Draw in four smaller triangles using the green slip.

14 The finished tiles are ready for biscuit firing prior to glazing and final firing.

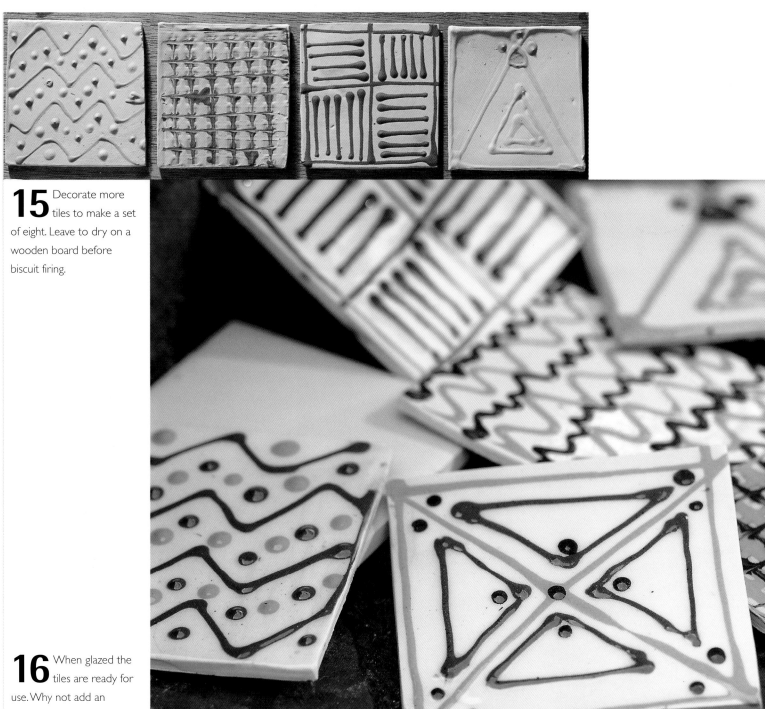

15 Decorate more tiles to make a set of eight. Leave to dry on a wooden board before biscuit firing.

16 When glazed the tiles are ready for use. Why not add an individual touch to your kitchen?

ikebana vase

Ikebana, the traditional Japanese art of flower arranging, relies on simplicity and natural forms for its effect. A slim vase is ideal for holding one or two stems or a single branch. Decorated in natural colors and textures, the vase complements an arrangement without overwhelming it.

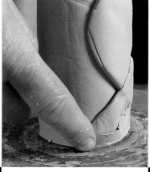

1 Roll a thick slab of clay (see Basic Techniques, on pages 20–27) and cut a small disk on a banding wheel as a base for the vase. Then roll a thinner slab and cut one edge straight, leaving the other uneven. Wrap the piece of clay around a rolling pin so that the rough edge overlaps the even one. Trim the base so that it is even.

2 Place the rolling pin and the vase centrally on the circular base of clay on the banding wheel.

3 Pull the clay up from the base to the body of the vase with your fingertips to join the two parts. Use a rubber kidney to smooth the surface of the vase, then roll it on a cloth to give an even texture.

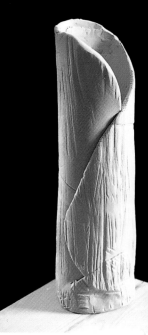

4 Apply more texture by pressing a piece of "corrugated" wood vertically against the vase.

5 Gently remove the rolling pin and leave the vase to dry before biscuit firing it.

6 Paint both the inside and outside of the vase in natural colors – blacks, grays, and ochers – painting up from the bottom to the top in the direction of the wood texture.

8 The decorated vase ready for glazing.

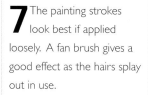

7 The painting strokes look best if applied loosely. A fan brush gives a good effect as the hairs splay out in use.

9 The vase is glazed inside and out to make it waterproof.

square box

Boxes provide lots of decorative possibilities. This small square one has a combed surface and embossed sprigs, finished with a simple colored slip outline. To make the box look professionally made, cut its components accurately and join them neatly to give a sharp profile.

tools and equipment

Linen or cotton sheeting

Battens

Rolling pin

Potter's knife

Metal kidney

Rubber kidney

Serrated metal modeling tool

Small natural sponge

Colored slip (red-brown)

Slip bottle

Sprigging tool

Cardboard template

1 Roll out a slab of clay (see Basic Techniques, on pages 20–27). Make sure that the slab is smooth and even, then use a cardboard template to cut six identical squares. The template used here measures 3½ inches square but you can make the box slightly bigger or smaller if you prefer.

2 Score around the edge of the square that will be the base of the box using a serrated metal modeling tool and a little slip.

3 Start assembling the sides of the box. Score down the edge of the side to be joined as you go. Push the first side down gently to make sure that it is standing square.

7 Roll a coil of clay for the handle. Texture it by pushing the edge of a piece of batten into it to give a rope effect.

4 Join the second and third sides. These will both overlap slightly and you will need to trim them and then smooth over the joints. The fourth side will be a short one, so measure and cut away any excess clay before assembling.

6 Cut two slab strips to fit inside the lid to keep it in place on the box. Use a serrated metal modeling tool and slip to score on the underside of the lid where the two strips are to be positioned. Score the edge of the two strips before firmly joining them to the lid.

5 Smooth all the joints and corners, first with a metal kidney then with a rubber kidney, for a neat finish to the edges.

8 Twist the coil and apply it to the lid. Push it down firmly at each end. Add a decorative feature to the ends of the coil by using a sprigging tool to give an embossed effect.

10 Fill a slip bottle with red-brown slip. Shake it gently to check that the end is filled and try out a trail on a piece of board. Then draw an outline in slip around the lid to frame it.

9 Texture the sides and lid of the box by combing a serrated metal modeling tool across the surface of the clay. Add a small ball of clay in the center of each side and repeat the embossed design with the sprig used for each end of the handle. This links the design of the box.

11 Do not worry if the line of slip looks a bit uneven on the textured surface – this is all part of the charm of this piece.

12 Draw slip lines around all the sides of the box. Leave to dry before biscuit firing.

13 Glaze the inside of the box first. Ladle the glaze in, swirl it around, then pour out to ensure an even coverage.

14 Dip the sides of the box into the glaze making sure you cover every surface.

15 Finally dip in the lid, holding it by the two strips on the underside.

16 The finished box is now ready for use.

bookends

This friendly bespectacled bookworm will take care of your favorite books and encourage even the most hesitant of readers. The bookends are simply two slabs of clay and the bookworm is made from a coil, then painted in bright primary colors. Have fun!

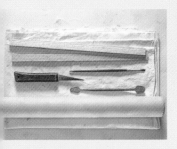

tools and equipment

Linen or cotton sheeting

Battens

Rolling pin

Potter's knife

Serrated metal modeling tool

Artist's brushes

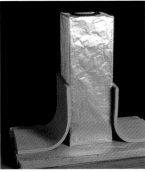

1 Roll out a slab of clay (see Basic Techniques, on pages 20–27). Then cut two rectangles the same size (those used here measure 10½ x 4½ inches). To shape the bookends, cover a box with foil and rest the slabs against the box. The sides of the bookends should be a little higher than the bases so that they balance. Try to shape them into a right angle with as little gap at the bottom as possible, but make sure that the clay does not crack.

2 Roll a thick coil for the worm. Start at the middle, and roll up then roll down the coil to get it even. If necessary roll the coil out on a board.

3 Roll the edge of a batten against the coil to make a spiral, segmented pattern for the worm.

4 Taper the end of the worm's tail by rolling it. Twist and flatten it slightly with the piece of wood.

6 Pull the cloth away to leave the texture on the surface of the clay.

5 Texture the whole of the worm by placing a coarse-woven cloth over it and rubbing over it with your fingers.

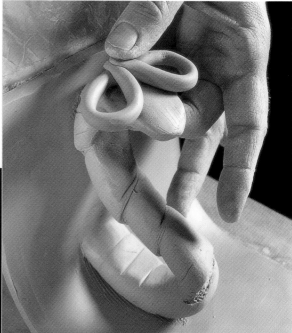

8 Flatten the head end of the coil to make it look like a worm's face. Score the other bookend at the top and bottom and join the coil. Attach the bottom part first, then loop the coil into an "S" shape so that the head pokes forward a little. Roll a thin coil and attach two small circles to the head for the worm's glasses.

7 Cut the worm in half at a 45-degree angle. Join the cut mitered end to the upright of the slab scoring the surface first. Loop the tail down, give it a little twist, and join it to the slab base about 2 inches from the end of the tail.

9 Cut a slit for a mouth with a knife. Push the end of an artist's brush through each spectacle to make an eye.

10 Leave the bookends to dry before biscuit firing.

11 Paint the worm in stripes using underglaze colors – yellow, blue, green, and red.

12 Paint the worm's spectacles black. Apply a thin line of black paint to its mouth.

13 Paint the bookends in blue.

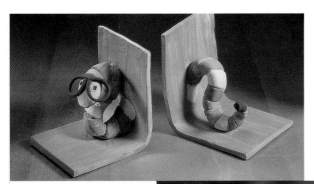

14 The finished bookends ready for glazing by dipping.

15 A close-up of the worm after it has been painted.

16 After glazing, the bookends are ready to hold a library of books.

game pieces

*T*raditional checkerboard games such as chess and checkers are popular with all ages. Using a set of pieces that you have made yourself will add to the enjoyment. Templates are provided here for the shapes, but you can adapt the design as you wish.

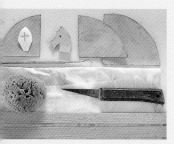
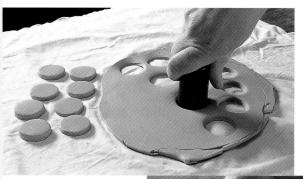

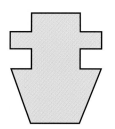

1 To make the checkers pieces, roll out a slab of clay (see Basic Techniques, on pages 20–27). Cut the pieces using a film canister with the end cut off – this allows you to gently push the clay through.

3 Carefully pry the toy wheel off the checkers piece to leave a perfect impression. Make a complete set of pieces using two colors of clay.

2 Roll the pieces along the sheeting to give a smooth, finished edge. Impress a toy wheel or similar circular object into the pieces, pushing it down evenly with your finger or banging it down with the end of a rolling pin.

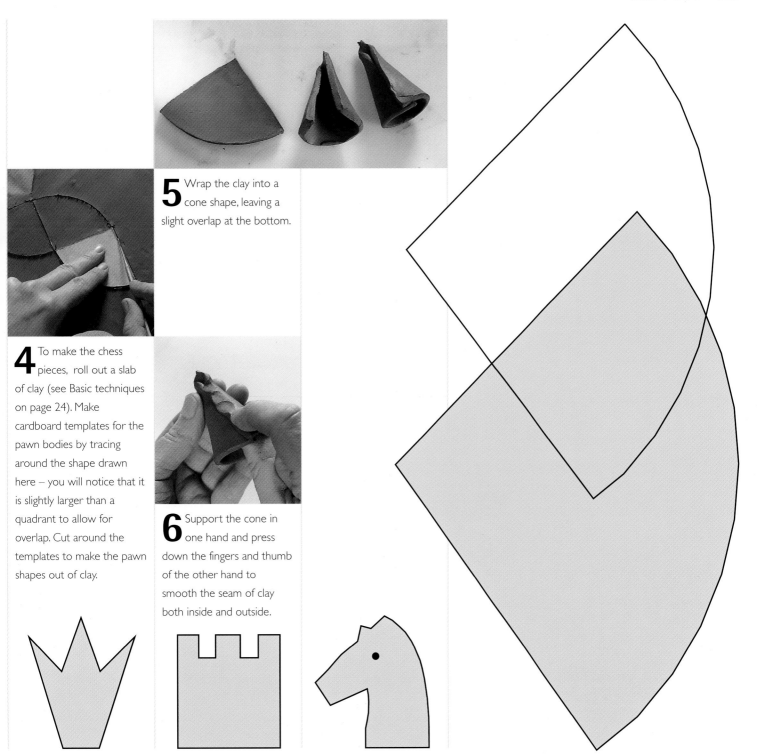

5 Wrap the clay into a cone shape, leaving a slight overlap at the bottom.

4 To make the chess pieces, roll out a slab of clay (see Basic techniques on page 24). Make cardboard templates for the pawn bodies by tracing around the shape drawn here – you will notice that it is slightly larger than a quadrant to allow for overlap. Cut around the templates to make the pawn shapes out of clay.

6 Support the cone in one hand and press down the fingers and thumb of the other hand to smooth the seam of clay both inside and outside.

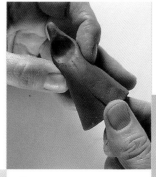

8 Pinch with your finger and thumb to make the top or head of the pawn. Indent the shoulders by pinching between your fingers – this makes the pieces easier to hold when moving them in a game.

7 Make the base flat by cutting it even with a knife, then bang it down to make sure it stands straight. Smooth the base between your fingers over a piece of sheeting.

10 Cut the tops off the bodies of the main pieces. Cut a split in the top of each piece, slide in the head shape and squeeze the clay together to complete. Neaten the pieces by smoothing the edges carefully between your fingers over sheeting.

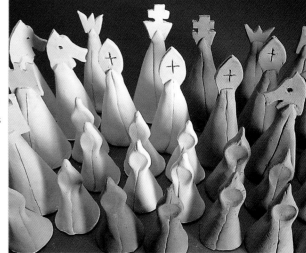

9 Make cardboard templates for the bodies and heads of the main pieces and use them to cut the shapes out of clay. Wrap and join the cones as in steps 5–7.

11 Make a complete set of pieces using two colors of clay. Leave to dry before biscuit firing.

12 The glazed chess pieces make a personal and unique set.

mirror frame

Seaside themes appeal to everyone and this small mirror frame will add a touch of style to any bathroom. This is a good way to make use of those seashells you gather on vacation, but you could copy this idea with similar small items that have a raised texture.

tools and equipment

- **Linen or cotton sheeting**
- **Battens**
- **Rolling pin**
- **Potter's knife**
- **Dentist's tool**
- **Serrated metal modeling tool**
- **Artist's brushes**
- **Seashells**
- **Cardboard templates**
- **Small natural sponge**

1 Make two cardboard templates, one measuring 1½ x 10 inches and the other measuring 1½ x 7½ inches. Roll out a slab of clay (see Basic Techniques, on pages 20–27), but make sure it is no thicker than ¼ inch or the frame will be too heavy to hang on the wall. Cut out two strips of clay from each template so that you have two long strips and two short ones.

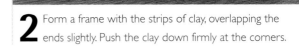

2 Form a frame with the strips of clay, overlapping the ends slightly. Push the clay down firmly at the corners.

3 Place a starfish on a slab of clay and cut around it. Place the top of the starfish onto the cut-out shape to obtain an accurate impression of the starfish.

5 Cut a thin ribbon of clay and twist it to represent seaweed. Lay out your design before placing the pieces on the frame. It is sometimes easier to sketch it out on paper first.

4 Cut a shell shape and press the cut-out clay onto a real seashell. Then bend the clay the other way with your finger to make a clay shell.

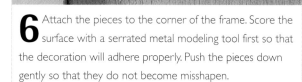

7 Overlaying the pieces a little gives a more interesting effect.

6 Attach the pieces to the corner of the frame. Score the surface with a serrated metal modeling tool first so that the decoration will adhere properly. Push the pieces down gently so that they do not become misshapen.

9 Use a dentist's tool to draw sea anemone shapes on a slab.

8 Balance the design by adding a starfish and a shell in other corners, remembering to score the surface of the frame first so that they are secure.

10 Cut out the flower shapes and decorate the corners by indenting them. These marks are produced with the end of an oriental brush, but use whatever you have to hand that is suitable.

11 Add the flower shapes to the frame. Vary the positions of the pieces. For instance, curve a shell upward to give more movement to the design.

12 Complete the decoration of the frame by adding seaside pieces to the sides.

13 Leave the frame to dry before biscuit firing it.

15 Use a brush to apply a thin wash of green to the ribbon seaweed. Paint in the areas underneath for a more three-dimensional effect.

14 Apply underglaze colors to the frame using a sponge for a light effect. The colors used here are pastel washes of yellow ocher, coral red, and lemon yellow, and the sponge is gently dipped into the color. Sponging allows subtle blending that gives depth to the shapes.

17 Make sure you follow the directions of the indentations on the shells when you are adding detail lines. Add a little blue to the corners for contrast.

18 The finished frame is ready for glazing.

16 Loosely paint in the details of the shells with black.

19 To hang the frame up, cut a piece of thick cardboard the same size and fix it to the frame with tile cement.

wheel thrown
pots

Onto the wheel! Here is where many people feel the real craft of the potter lies. However, it is just one of many methods to shape clay. Controlling a lump of clay on the wheel and turning it into a well-shaped pot may not be a skill that you acquire immediately. Learning to do so, however, is great fun and you will feel an enormous sense of achievement as you progress. Throwing is a gradual process of practicing techniques and then building on your triumphs.

Six basic pots are presented here – a bowl with a foot, a plate, a vase, a ginger jar, a mug, and a jug. They will introduce you to throwing rounded, flat, and cylinder shapes and show you how to make a foot for a bowl, a rim, a lid, a handle, and a pouring lip.

bowl

Here is a bowl to start you potting on the wheel. It is a simple, classic shape and involves basic centering and throwing techniques, so you can produce a real pot while you are learning! A foot is added to "lift" the pot and the decoration was inspired by a Japanese kimono.

tools and equipment

Metal turning tools

Wooden modeling tools

Serrated metal modeling tool

Small natural sponge

Chamois

Cheesewire

1 Use a prepared ball of clay weighing about 1 pound (see Equipment and Materials, on pages 8–19). Center the clay on the wheel, bringing it up into a cone and down again until you are happy that the clay is balanced and there are no air bubbles (see Basic Techniques, on pages 20–27). Make a hollow in the clay and open up the bowl by pushing in your fingers and using the other hand to guide the shape. Start to raise the sides of the pot by pushing in at the base to pull the clay up.

2 Gently pull the sides of the bowl up and outward with your fingers. The fingers inside exert the most pressure, while the outside hand still guides the shape. Using a sponge will help you to do this more smoothly.

3 Smooth the edge of the rim using the thumb and forefinger of one hand in a gentle pinching action and the gap between the forefinger and middle finger of the other hand. This action also helps to prevent any air bubbles.

8 Slide the bowl off the wheel using the first two fingers of each hand in a scissors shape. This will ensure you do not distort the bowl.

4 Flatten the rim by pinching gently with the thumb and forefinger of one hand and pushing down carefully on top with the forefinger of the other.

6 Use a sponge to remove any excess water inside the pot.

7 Slice the bowl from the wheel using a cheesewire. Wet the wheel a little to slide the bowl off (it should not be overwet or the base may crack later). When you have more experience in making small pots you may find it easier to lift them off the wheel with two hands.

5 Define the rim with the nail of your forefinger. Use the first two fingers of your other hand inside the pot to keep the line steady.

9 Leave the bowl to dry until the clay is just leather hard. It can then be turned if you wish to add a foot to it.

13 Trim the outside of the bowl so that you are happy with the shape. Go to step 19.

11 Carefully turn off the excess clay with a metal turning tool. Never attempt to turn the inside of a bowl – you should always leave enough clay at the base to turn a foot that will harmonize with the shape of the bowl.

10 Turn the pot upside down and center it on the wheel to make a foot. Place three small balls of clay to hold it secure. There are two ways of adding a foot to a pot – by turning or by adding a coil. If you wish to add a coil foot, go to step 14. If you wish to turn the foot, first make a line with your fingernail to mark the position of its outer circumference. Hold your hand steady by pushing it down with the other hand.

12 Turn away any excess clay from inside the foot of the bowl.

14 If you are adding a coil foot, you should first turn the bowl to the shape you wish by trimming clay away with a metal turning tool.

16 Roll a coil of moist clay for the foot. Join the coil to the base of the bowl, pushing down firmly as you go.

18 Neaten the profile of the bowl with the end of a wooden modeling tool.

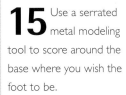

15 Use a serrated metal modeling tool to score around the base where you wish the foot to be.

17 Shape the coil foot with your fingers. Then smooth it with a chamois. Flatten the rim of the foot by pinching gently with the thumb and forefinger of one hand and pushing down carefully on top with the forefinger of the other.

19 Leave the bowl to dry before you start biscuit firing.

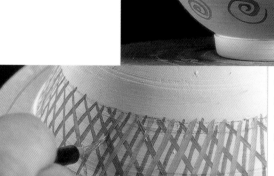

21 Start painting the design inside the bowl. Remember that the colors will change during firing. When you have painted the inside, paint the rim of the bowl.

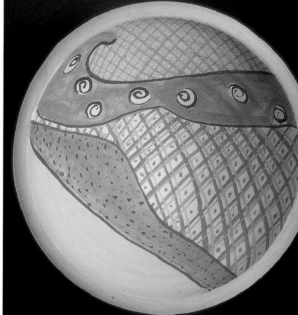

23 View of the side of the bowl before firing. The foot is left plain to act as a contrast against the colored design.

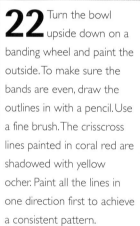

20 When the bowl has been biscuit fired, you can start to paint it with underglaze colors. Draw the design inside with a pencil – the carbon will burn off during the firing process. You can sketch your design out on paper first, but remember you will be working on a curved surface.

22 Turn the bowl upside down on a banding wheel and paint the outside. To make sure the bands are even, draw the outlines in with a pencil. Use a fine brush. The crisscross lines painted in coral red are shadowed with yellow ocher. Paint all the lines in one direction first to achieve a consistent pattern.

24 View of the inside of the bowl before firing.

25 Glaze the bowl to change and enhance the colors of the paints.

plate

To make this plate you will need to fix a batt onto the wheel as it requires a fairly large surface. This also enables you to remove the pot from the wheel easily. The plate is decorated with a fish design by "drawing" on it with colored slip. You could "write" a calligraphic pattern if you wished.

tools and equipment

Batt

Small natural sponge

Chamois

Wooden modeling tool

Potter's knife

Cheesewire

Throwing rib (or old credit card)

Colored slips and slip bottle

Sponge stick

1 To secure the batt to the wheel, first throw a ball of clay on the wheel so that it is rather like a plate. Then make ridges with the fingers of one hand, holding your wrist steady with your other hand. You can also buy wheels that have three locating pins to take a batt.

2 Place the batt on the wheel, pushing down firmly so that it is secure. The batt needs to be quite dry underneath to stick to the clay. It also needs to be dry on top as that will be the throwing area. Wipe it off with a damp sponge.

3 Center a prepared ball of clay weighing about 1½ pounds (see Basic Techniques, on pages 20–27).

4 As you are throwing a large surface it is important to make the base even right across the plate. Use the palm of your hand to draw the base out, holding the wrist steady with the other hand.

5 Stop the wheel and check the depth of the plate with a potter's knife. Also prick any air bubbles that are likely to occur when working on a large area.

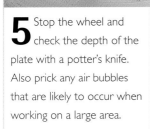

6 Push out the rim using the tips of your fingers. Again hold your wrist steady with your other hand.

7 Push with your fingers until the plate is the diameter you require.

8 Raise the clay from the bottom between your fingers to make an edge to the plate. Form a rim between your fingertips.

9 Use an old credit card or throwing rib to neaten the plate off and give a smooth surface.

10 When the clay has dried out, apply the fish decoration with yellow ocher slip. Make sure that the tip of the slip bottle is filled and that the slip is of the correct consistency by making a practice trail on a piece of board. The leaves of the water weed are applied by dipping the end of a sponge stick into green slip. The plate is now ready for biscuit firing.

11 The plate is finished with a clear glaze.

vase

This bright vase will give you a chance to practice "bellying out" to make a rounded, closed space. The decoration is achieved by scraping a wooden modeling tool upward to incise vertical lines. A bought colored brush-on glaze saves the problem of mixing a glaze to a recipe.

tools and equipment

Chamois

Bamboo turning tool

Wooden modeling tool

Cheesewire

Small natural sponge

Sponge stick

1 Use a prepared ball of clay weighing about ¾ pound (see Equipment and Materials, on pages 8–19). Center the clay on the wheel, bringing it up into a cone and down again until you are happy that the clay is balanced and there are no air bubbles (see Basic Techniques, on pages 20–27).

3 Start to shape the sides of the pot, guiding it up into a cone shape between the first two fingers of one hand and the knuckle of the forefinger of the other hand.

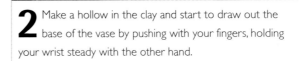

2 Make a hollow in the clay and start to draw out the base of the vase by pushing with your fingers, holding your wrist steady with the other hand.

4 Continue to raise the pot, pulling the clay up from the base to the top. Aim for an even thickness of clay, though the top of the pot may be a little thicker.

6 Belly out the rounded shape of the vase by guiding with your fingers inside the pot. Use the fingers of the other hand as a support on the outside.

8 Clean the base of the pot by trimming away excess clay with a bamboo turning tool. Then clean and define the profile of the vase by trimming away excess clay from the sides with a bamboo turning tool.

5 "Collar" the neck of the vase in, drawing it in at the top by gently guiding it in with both hands.

7 Define the shape of the rim with your fingernail, holding your forefinger upright just below the top of the pot. Then smooth the rim with a chamois leather held between your thumb and forefinger.

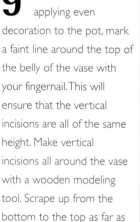

10 Use the point of the modeling tool to achieve a clean shape to each incision.

9 As a guide to applying even decoration to the pot, mark a faint line around the top of the belly of the vase with your fingernail. This will ensure that the vertical incisions are all of the same height. Make vertical incisions all around the vase with a wooden modeling tool. Scrape up from the bottom to the top as far as the marked line, using the fingers of the other hand inside the pot to steady it.

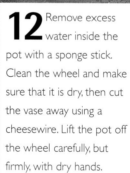

11 Clean and define the rim of the vase with the end of a wooden modeling tool. You can turn this into a decorative feature by trimming to create a wide flat band. Make a decorative ridge with the end of the modeling tool at the top of the incised lines. Use the line made by your fingernail as a guide line.

12 Remove excess water inside the pot with a sponge stick. Clean the wheel and make sure that it is dry, then cut the vase away using a cheesewire. Lift the pot off the wheel carefully, but firmly, with dry hands.

13 Leave the vase to dry before you begin biscuit firing.

14 Use a ready-made brush-on glaze to decorate the vase, shaking the bottle well first. A plain colored glaze will enhance the ridged lines on the pot. Pour glaze into the vase, then swirl it around and use a brush to glaze the inside of the vase. Tip any excess glaze back into its original container.

15 Brush the glaze onto the outside of the vase. Do this on a banding wheel, but make sure you clean any drips of glaze off the wheel afterward. Do not handle the vase until it is dry.

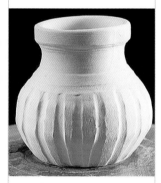

16 The glazed vase before firing. Clean any glaze off the bottom of the pot so that it will not stick to the kiln.

17 This vase shows effective use of a colored glaze.

ginger **jar**

Attractive jars of all kinds are always useful. This ginger jar is made with a turned mushroom lid with a knob. An incised decoration is worked into the clay with a piece of corrugated wood and bands of color are painted on, linking the design of the jar with the lid.

tools and equipment

Wooden turning tool with string

Calipers

Corrugated wood

Throwing rib (or old credit card)

Small natural sponge

Chamois

Cheesewire

Metal turning tool

Banding wheel (or cake turntable)

1 Use a prepared ball of clay weighing about 1 pound (see Equipment and Materials, on pages 8–19). Center the clay on the wheel (see Basic Techniques, on pages 20–27). Then make a hollow in the clay and draw out the base of the vase by pushing with your fingers, holding your wrist steady with the other hand. Shape the sides of the pot, guiding it upward with your fingertips. Then, with your fingers inside and supporting the shape on the outside with your other hand, belly out the pot to round the shape.

2 Continue to raise the pot, pulling the clay up from the base to the top. When it is the required height, press the clay down at the top to form an inner rim to take a lid. Do this with a gentle pinching action between the fingertips and thumb of one hand, supporting the shape on the outside of the pot with the tip of the forefinger of your other hand. To add a mushroom lid with a knob, press the rim down slightly to give a curved shape on which it can sit.

3 If you find any air bubbles in the clay, prick them with the point of a knife or a needle.

7 Leave the jar to dry before making the lid.

4 Form the neck of the jar by pinching the top of the pot between the thumb and forefinger of one hand and pushing the tip of the forefinger of your other hand on the outside of the pot. Smooth and define the outside of the jar with an old credit card.

5 Incise a wavy line decoration around the jar with a piece of corrugated wood. Support the pot inside with the fingers of your other hand.

6 Measure the inside diameter of the jar with calipers so that you can make the correct size lid.

9 Form a lid by depressing your finger to leave a knob in the center of the clay. Use your other hand to steady the clay.

8 To turn a lid with a knob of clay, you need first to throw a hump of clay. Do this by centering the clay and bringing it up into a cone shape.

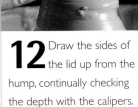

10 Define the profile of the knob and lid with your fingertips.

11 Measure the diameter of the lid with calipers to check that it will fit the top of the jar. Adjust the size of the lid by trimming or further shaping outward if necessary.

12 Draw the sides of the lid up from the hump, continually checking the depth with the calipers.

13 Use a wooden turning tool to mark a line in the hump at the required depth.

16 Place a ring of moist clay on the wheel to rest the lid on upside down. Place the lid upside down on the ring of clay. Then use a metal turning tool to trim it into the shape you require.

14 Wrap the string on the end of the turning tool all around the line.

15 Hold the lid between the first two fingers of one hand and pull the string with your other hand while the wheel is gently turning. Lift off the lid. Leave to dry a little.

17 Remove the lid to dry before biscuit firing and decorating the jar.

18 You can decorate the jar when it has been biscuited. Paint it with bands of underglaze colors, placing it on a banding wheel to make working easier. Paint the combed area in green, then outline it in yellow. The jar is painted in only two colors for a more striking effect.

19 Outline the yellow bands with green.

20 Paint the lid to match the design of the jar. Paint the knob green.

21 Outline the inner rim of the lid in yellow paint.

22 Paint the rim of the lid green.

23 Paint the rim of the jar yellow. Finish the decoration by adding a wider yellow band further down the pot and a final green outlining stripe near the bottom.

24 Leave the jar to dry before glazing.

25 Glaze the outside of the jar by plunging it upright into the glaze bucket, flexing out your fingers inside the pot to grip it. Give it a little twist to shake off any drips.

26 Glaze the inside of the jar by ladling the glaze in. Pour out the excess at an angle, again twisting the pot with a little shake to loosen any drips.

27 Finish off any finger marks or missed areas with a brush.

28 Similarly glaze the lid by dipping it into the glaze bucket.

29 Clean glaze from the base of the pot so that it will not stick when it is put in the kiln.

30 This traditional ginger jar can be used for storage or as an attractive decorative pot.

mug

Drinking from a mug you have made yourself adds a certain quality to your coffee, tea, or hot chocolate! Mugs also make useful gifts and you can decorate them to suit your own friends' preferences in color and style. In this project you will learn how to pull a handle.

tools and equipment

Wooden turning tool

Serrated metal modeling tool

Throwing rib (or old credit card)

Cheesewire

Small natural sponge

Chamois

Sprigging tool

1 Use a prepared ball of clay weighing about ¾ pound (see Equipment and Materials, on pages 8–19). Center the clay on the wheel, bringing it up into a cone and down again until you are happy that the clay is balanced and there are no air bubbles (see Basic Techniques, on pages 20–27). Make a hollow in the clay and open up the pot by pushing in your fingers and using your other hand to guide the shape. Start to raise the sides of the mug by pushing in at the base to pull the clay up, then gently pull them up (see Bowl project, on pages 114–119).

2 Define and smooth the edge of the rim using the thumb and forefinger of one hand in a gentle pinching action and the gap between the forefinger and middle finger of the other hand. Shape the foot of the mug by removing excess clay at the base with a wooden turning tool. Leave it fairly broad to give solidity to the mug. An old credit card is useful for smoothing off the surface.

3 Smooth with a sponge and a chamois. Take extra care with the rim because people will drink from it. Also make sure it is not too thick.

4 Incise a vertical line pattern with a serrated metal modeling tool, supporting the pot inside with your other hand.

5 If you find that you have pushed the top of the mug out of shape, gently correct it with your fingers.

9 Make a double groove pattern in the handle by running your thumb down each side of the clay.

7 Moisten your other hand by dipping it in water and gently start to draw down the clay.

6 To pull a handle, first take a lump of well-wedged clay and roll it into a thick sausage shape. Hold it firmly in one hand toward the top end.

8 Pull down in continuous movements, gradually lengthening and flattening the handle.

10 Once the handle is a reasonable length cut off the clay by using your first two fingers in a scissors movement.

11 Shape the clay into a handle shape and leave to settle and dry on a board for a short time.

13 Moisten your fingers, then press the handle into place, holding it lightly in the other hand. Smooth it at the joints with thumb and fingers.

15 Push the end of the sprigging tool into the ball of clay to indent the pattern, supporting the other side if necessary.

12 Scratch the top and bottom of the mug where you want the handle to fit. This will provide a key so that the clay will adhere together properly.

17 After the biscuit firing, paint the rim of the mug in blue. Do this on a banding wheel for a more even effect, using just one stroke, but be careful that the wheel does not revolve too fast. Remember that cobalt blue looks mauve when applied as a wash and will change color after firing.

16 This sprigging tool has produced a simple embossed pattern that looks very attractive. Leave the mug to dry before biscuit firing.

14 To make a sprig decoration, place a small ball of clay on the side of the mug.

18 Paint blue vertical stripes on the incised lines to match the rim. Use the brush in an upward stroke.

19 Paint the embossed sprig. If you wish you could paint the foot in brown to contrast with the colors of the mug. Then glaze the mug (see Firing and Glazing, on pages 34–43).

20 The finished mug, after glazing and firing, can now be used to drink from.

jug

This jug is a basic cylinder shape that is bellied out. It is important to make a good lip so that the jug pours well. The handle is placed so that it balances the shape of the pot – think in terms of a rather large person with hands on hips!

tools and equipment

Wooden turning tool

Serrated metal turning tool

Cheesewire

Throwing rib (or old credit card)

Small natural sponge

Chamois

1 Use a prepared ball of clay weighing about 2 pounds (see Equipment and Materials, on pages 8–19). Center the clay on the wheel, bringing it up into a cone and down again until you are happy that the clay is balanced and there are no air bubbles (see Basic Techniques, on pages 20–27). Make a hollow in the clay and start to pull out the base of the jug with your fingers.

2 Start to shape the sides of the pot, pulling the clay up from the base to the top to form a cylinder. Use a sponge to do this smoothly.

3 Belly out the pot with your fingers inside the jug. Your outside hand follows just behind the inside one to affirm the shape. Again, use a sponge on the outside to do this smoothly.

5 Finish shaping and smoothing the pot with a throwing rib or old credit card. Define the profile of the neck and belly.

8 Turn off any excess clay from the base with a wooden turning tool to form a sturdy foot.

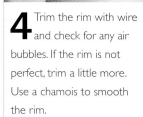

4 Trim the rim with wire and check for any air bubbles. If the rim is not perfect, trim a little more. Use a chamois to smooth the rim.

7 Form the spout by pressing the pulled-up area between your thumb and forefinger on the outside of the pot, gently pushing out the shape from inside with the knuckle of the other forefinger.

6 To start the lip, gently pull up a small area of the rim by stroking it between your finger and thumb. Once it is evenly pulled up, smooth the whole rim with a chamois.

9 Leave the jug to dry slightly on a batt. Meanwhile form a handle (see Mug project, on pages 134–137).

11 Join the handle at the bottom and smooth the joints with a sponge.

14 Start to paint the jug, holding it inside with one hand and supporting it on your knee. Choose a design that will enhance the jug – for instance, tall flowers are suitable for a tall jug. Here, sprays of delphiniums are painted up from the bottom to the top in cobalt blue. Each flower is simply a series of petals, worked slightly smaller each time toward the top.

13 Leave the jug to dry before biscuit firing.

10 Use a serrated metal modeling tool to scratch the surface of the pot at the top and bottom of the jug where you wish to place the handle (opposite the spout!). The bottom of the handle should be about halfway down the body of the jug. Moisten your fingers, then push the top of the handle onto the jug, holding the pot firmly in your other hand.

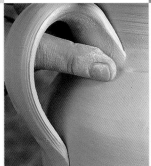

12 Smooth both top and bottom joints on the handle with your finger.

15 Turn the pot upside down to paint in the leaves. You may wish to mix greens to achieve the right tones. Paint the leaves and stalks with long downward strokes, making sure that the stalks are joined to the flowers and that the leaves are joined to the stalks.

16 With the jug still upside down, paint in lupins between the delphiniums. Mix a little deep pink with cornflower blue to make a mauve color, then apply the petals by simply pressing down the length of the bristles. Work downward, making the petals slightly smaller in size as you go.

17 Place the jug on a banding wheel and paint the rim in cobalt blue. Finally, add a line around the base to define the foot.

18 The decorated jug ready for glazing.

19 Pour the glaze into the jug, swirl it around, then pour it out at an angle. Twist the pot and give it a little shake to loosen any drips.

20 Dip the jug into the glaze, flexing your fingers outward inside the pot.

index

Acknowledgments

The authors would like to thank the following:

Bath Potters' Supplies

2 Dorset Close

Bath

BA2 3RF

01225 337046

Potclays Limited

Brickkiln Lane

Etruria

Stoke-on-Trent

ST4 7BP

01782 219816

John Melville for his help and patience. Margaret MacEvoy for all her help and advice.
Jenny Rawlings for all her help and advice. Jo Norris for her help and support.
Andy Lloyd Wiliams for help and advice.

Richard Green, furnituremaker

Somerleaze Farm

Coal Lane

Hopsford

Somerset

For wood shavings for tree decoration photograph